INSIGHT POCKET GUIDE

PERTH

D0308399

Discovery
CHANNEL

APA PUBLICATIONS
Part of the Langenscheidt Publishing Group
L

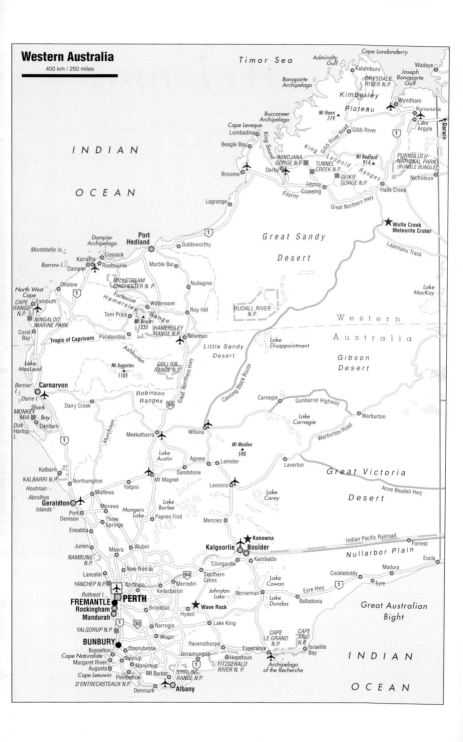

Western Australia

400 km / 250 miles

Timor Sea

INDIAN

OCEAN

Cape Londonderry
Admiralty Gulf
Kalumburu
Wadaye
Joseph Bonaparte Gulf
DRYSDALE RIVER N.P.
Bonaparte Archipelago
Kimberley Plateau
Wyndham
Kununurra
Mt Honn 779
Lake Argyle
Darwin

Buccaneer Archipelago
Cape Leveque
Lombadina
Gibb River Road
Gibb River
King Sound
Beagle Bay
Leopold Ranges
Mt Bedford 914
PURNULULU NATIONAL PARK (BUNGLE BUNGLE)
Broome
WINDJANA GORGE N.P.
Derby
TUNNEL CREEK N.P.
GEIKIE GORGE N.P.
Nicholson
Fitzroy
Fitzroy Crossing
Halls Creek
Lagrange
Great Northern Hwy

Wolfe Creek Meteorite Crater

Dampier Archipelago
Port Hedland
Goldsworthy
Great Sandy Desert
Lajamanu Track
Montebello Is.
Karratha
Cossack
Barrow I.
Dampier
Roebourne
Marble Bar
Nullagine
North West Cape
Onslow
MILLSTREAM CHICHESTER N.P.
Lake MacKay
CAPE RANGE N.P.
Exmouth
Forfescue
Withenoom
Roy Hill
RUDALL RIVER N.P.
NINGALOO MARINE PARK
Hamersley Range
Tom Price
Mt Bruce 1235
HAMERSLEY RANGE N.P.
Western
Coral Bay
Tropic of Capricorn
Paraburdoo
Newman
Australia
Lake MacLeod
Ashburton
Little Sandy Desert
Lake Disappointment
Gibson Desert
Bernier I.
Mt Augustus 1105
COLLIER RANGE N.P.
Dorre I.
Robinson Ranges
Shark
Canning Stock Route
MONKEY MIA
Bay
Denham
Dairy Creek
Carnegie
Gunbarrel Highway
Dirk Hartog I.
Murchison
Lake Carnegie
Warburton
Meekatharra
Wiluna
Warburton Road
Kalbarri
Mt Maiden 590
Great Victoria
KALBARRI N.P.
Northampton
Lake Austin
Agnew
Leinster
Houtman
Mullewa
Yalgoo
Mt Magnet
Sandstone
Laverton
Desert
Abrolhos Islands
Geraldton
Morawa
Leonora
Anne Beadell Hwy
Port Denison
Three Springs
Mongers Lake
Paynes Find
Lake Barlee
Lake Carey
Eneabba
Menzies
Jurien
Moora
Wubin
Indian Pacific Railroad
Forrest
NAMBUNG N.P.
Lancelin
New Norcia
Coolgardie
Kanowna
Kalgoorlie
Boulder
Kambalda
Nullarbor Plain
Eucla
Cocklebiddy
Madura
YANCHEP N.P.
Northam
Merredin
Southern Cross
Lake Cowan
Eyre
Rottnest I.
FREMANTLE
PERTH
Kellerberrin
Johnston Lake
Norseman
Eyre Hwy
Rockingham
Mandurah
Brookton
Hyden
Wave Rock
Lake Dundas
Balladonia
Great Australian Bight
YALGORUP N.P.
Narrogin
Lake King
BUNBURY
Wagin
CAPE LE GRAND N.P.
CAPE ARID N.P.
Busselton
Donnybrook
Ravensthorpe
Esperance
Israelite Bay
Cape Naturaliste
Nannup
Jerramungup
Hopetoun
Margaret River
Manjimup
FITZGERALD RIVER N.P.
Archipelago of the Recherche
Augusta
Mt Barker
STIRLING RANGE N.P.
INDIAN
Cape Leeuwin
Pemberton
D'ENTRECASTEAUX N.P.
Denmark
Albany
OCEAN

introduction

Welcome

This guidebook combines the interests and enthusiasms of two of the world's best-known information providers: Insight Guides, who have set the standard for visual travel guides since 1970, and Discovery Channel, the world's premier source of non-fiction television programming. Its aim is to bring you the best of Perth and its surroundings in a series of tailor-made itineraries devised by Insight's Perth correspondent, Vic Waters.

Perth, the capital of Western Australia, is the world's remotest city, closer to Bali, Indonesia, than it is to Sydney. Its attractions, however, are anything but remote: there are historic buildings and world-class museums, picturesque parks and gardens, some of Australia's best restaurants, beaches like Cottesloe and the wildlife reserve of Rottnest Island, the funky port city of Fremantle, wine tasting in Swan Valley and Margaret River – and more. This book captures the city and its environs in a series of walking and driving itineraries, and includes excursions to places outside of Perth. Complementing the itineraries are chapters on shopping, eating out and nightlife, plus a calendar of special events and a fact-packed practical information section which includes a list of recommended hotels.

Vic Waters, a journalist, writer and photographer, was a devoted Londoner until he visited Perth in 1989. Years later, he's still there, trapped by the glorious year-round sunshine and the easy-going Aussie lifestyle. 'Perth still feels like a holiday town," he says, 'although it's a modern multicultural city and capital of one-third of the vast Australian continent. Sure, we're in touch with the world, but that buffer of ocean and bush keeps the world at a comfortable arm's length.' For Waters, a dedicated sports junkie, Perth's beaches, rivers and parks make it a perfect spot to test his athletic prowess. In fact, more than a decade of running and racing in and around Perth makes him more than amply qualified to recommend the itineraries in this guide.

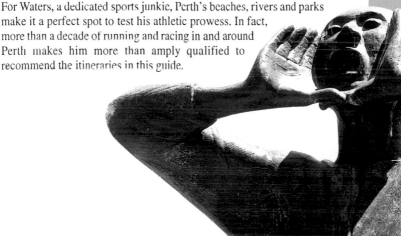

HISTORY AND CULTURE

From the time British soldiers first landed, to the migration of convict labour, the gold rush era and the city's modern-day political and social changes, this is a capsule account of Perth's chequered history**...............11**

CITY ITINERARIES

The first three itineraries cover Perth city's essential sights in detail. The following six explore other interesting areas and aspects of the city as well as its immediate surroundings.

Preceding pages: city view from Kings Park
Following pages: surf carnival at Leighton Beach

History *& Culture*

A t least 40,000 years before Europeans reached Australia, Aboriginal people flourished in the continent's west, their culture sustained by harmonious living with the land and nature. Europeans were first recorded as having visited the western shores in early 17th century. Dutchman Dirk Hartog was known to have landed near Carnarvon in 1616, followed by sailors from Holland, France and England. Another Dutch, Willen de Vlamingh, first ventured up the Swan River in January 1697, naming the river after the black swans – now a symbol of Western Australia (WA).

Colonial Settlement

The first settlement came from Britain's eastern Australian base. In 1826, French ships were sighted sailing around the western and southern coasts. Fearing they might try to settle, a British expedition from Sydney set up a military outpost at King George Sound on the south coast. It was more a 'spoiling action' than a permanent settlement, and in 1831 Major Edmund Lockyer and his group of soldiers and convicts were recalled to Sydney.

That same year, another Briton, Captain James Stirling, also set sail from New South Wales. He explored the west coast and suggested a Swan River colony. The territory was formally claimed on 2 May 1829, when Captain Charles Howe Fremantle landed in the Swan estuary to plant the Union Jack. In June, Stirling and 68 settlers arrived to found the Swan River Colony, naming it Perth to honour Sir George Murray, Britain's secretary of state for war and the colonies, born in Perthshire, Scotland. The port was named after Captain Fremantle.

Perth's site was chosen for its access to likely agricultural land and its location on the commercial route to the ocean, while being safe from naval shelling. The colony was planned as a money-maker, and investors, including Stirling, were encouraged with generous land grant terms.

The west was explored continuously from 1837, when George Grey landed at Hanover Bay and was thwarted by Aborigines, who drove his party back to their ship. Two years later, he landed at Shark Bay, and with 11 others walked to Perth. They lost one man on the way, withstood native attacks, and discovered and named many rivers on the route south. Such explorers are now immortalised, and names like Eyre, Roe and Forrest are perpetuated on roads, buildings and parks across the state.

Settlers followed in their wake, but when they moved into traditional tribal lands and hunting grounds they provoked murderous conflict with the original inhabitants. The local Aborigine community around Perth soon declined. The statue of Yagan – warrior leader of Aborigines, killed in 1833 – now

Left: John Forrest, early explorer of Perth
Right: statue of Yagan, Aboriginal warrior leader

stands on Heirisson Island as a silent reminder of those turbulent years. After 2 centuries of white settlement, Aboriginal tradition has been virtually extinguished, surviving in its pure form only in the more remote regions.

Perth's first settlers were British, in an outpost of empire. To them, independence from the old country would have been unthinkable. Today, the mindset has changed, even in Perth, which still has Australia's highest proportion of migrants from the British Isles. Since World War II, waves of migration, mainly from Europe and Asia, have created a multi-cultural population of Australians. Although a historic constitutional referendum held in November 1999 resulted in 54 percent of Australians voting to retain the monarchical arrangement, observers feel that it's only a matter of time before the country makes the transition to a republic.

Convict Era

Perth's population grew slowly until gold was found; the numbers then soared, from 46,000 in 1890 to 184,000 in 1901. In 1910, 282,000 people lived in the west – 38 percent of them in Perth. The trend has continued: most Australians cling to the shore in cities. Today, Perth is home to 1.3 million of WA's 1.8 million people.

In 1848, 41,622 people lived in the new colony. Labour shortage led to convicts being sent out from Britain, although transportation to the eastern states had ended in 1840. In WA's convict era (1850–60), prisoners built much of the early infrastructure: city buildings such as Government House, Perth Town Hall, the Cloisters and dozens more, as well as police stations, court houses, roads and bridges in the state's south-west. Ironically, they built Fremantle jail, and a smaller one in Perth. Convict presence made the citizenry nervous. Many carried guns by day, and didn't venture far at night.

Above: an aboriginal camp in WA, circa 1890
Left: ceremony at Perth's Government House

In 1856, Queen Victoria granted Perth city status, and in 1870, representative government was gained and the colony consolidated. People strolled and shopped at night under mid-80s street lighting, and enjoyed the Esplanade leisure area reclaimed from the Swan. Later, in the 1930s, a Depression-fighting reclamation project created Langley Park and Riverside Drive, and in 1954-8 the motor car era gobbled more river for the Narrows Bridge and Freeway.

Advent of the Railway

From the 1880s rail was king, opening up WA. The first government railway line was laid in 1879, north of Perth, carrying copper and lead from Northampton's mines to Geraldton's port. Two years later, rails linked Perth, Fremantle and Guildford. In 1898, they radiated south to Albany, north to Geraldton and, of course, east to Kalgoorlie and the Golden Mile.

In 1907, a 'Rescue Special' set a line speed record that stood for 47 years, when Fremantle divers dashed east to Coolgardie and saved a miner trapped for 9 days in a flooded goldmine at Bonnievale. It wasn't the first time Fremantle and the railways combined in a mercy dash. When the Pensioner Barracks caught fire in 1887, the Fremantle fire engine was loaded onto a train and rushed to aid the Perth brigade in saving the soldiers' quarters. Travel to the eastern states became easier in 1917, when the Trans-Australian Railway ran from Kalgoorlie to Port Augusta in south Australia.

Civil air travel began in 1944 and international flights in 1952, from Maylands airport in east Perth. But the world's first long-distance air service began in the early 1920s, flying off the reclaimed Langley Park just metres from the city centre. Small planes and helicopters still fly from there occasionally, and Maylands gave way to Perth's present domestic and international airports in 1963.

Gold

Gold discoveries in the late 1880s, and most importantly in the 1890s, were instrumental in the making of Perth. Stirling's 1827 report on the potential colony was optimistic about mining and he was finally proven right. Mining became a bedrock industry for city and state and remains so, contributing 75 percent of WA's multi-billion-dollar exports.

In 1862, a government reward of £5,000 was offered for discovery of a payable goldfield. Payout came in the 1880s with a strike in the state's far north, at Halls Creek in the Kimberley region. The Kimberley boom was short-lived but it inspired prospectors to scour the state. They made rich discoveries in the Pilbara, Yilgan and Murchison, but all were topped by Paddy Hannan and his partners, Tom Flanagan and Dan Shea. Their 1893 Kalgoorlie strike made the area famous as 'The Golden Mile'. Australia's eastern states were in depression and the WA 'cinderella' became the queen of colonies. Migrants flooded into Perth and business prospered.

Right: gold prospectors at Halls Creek, Kimberly

Infrastructure

Gold financed Perth's progress. In 1890, £87,000 worth of the precious metal was exported. Ten years on, it reached almost £4 million. More roads, drains, sewerage and lighting were installed and the population spilled out into new suburbs, some linked to the city by trams. More public transport changed the 'pedestrian' feel of Perth; by the 1920s, motor taxis and later, cars completed the transformation.

Road building accelerated in keeping with Perth's prosperity, prompting the *London Evening Standard* in 1906 to praise the city for its 'modern appliances for expediting communication either by road or car', and say that

'Perth put to utter shame the roadways of many far more pretentious and incomparably older towns and cities . . . both in the motherland and the United States'.

Quite an advance. In 1834, St Georges Terrace – Perth's first and most prestigious street – was a narrow clay-base strip; the first rickety timber causeway stretching across the Swan via Heirisson Island made its appearance a few years later. In the late 1870s, only parts of the central streets were 'macadamised' (with tarmac), and all the rest made of unsealed stone. In 1907, however, Perth had 90 miles of made roads, many sealed with tar, and by 1913, motor vehicles just about equalled the carts and carriages on its streets.

The era also created many of the neo-classical facades preserved today, such as His Majesty's Theatre and the Palace Hotel, now a bank. In 1895, the Palace was state-of-the-art, favoured in its heyday even by visiting federal politicians. Created by a Californian, John de Baun, it boasted 130 guest rooms, 12 baths (with hot and cold water), a library, a smoking/reading room, billiards, a post and telegraph office, electricity and an electric elevator, and 70 staff.

Government

Through the 1890s WA was self-governing, run by a ministry headed by Sir John Forrest. Among its actions was the 1898 Free Education Bill, although school had been compulsory since 1871 for children aged 6 to 14.

Women were given the vote in 1899. WA was a pioneer of female suffrage, ahead of Canada (1917), Britain (1918) and the USA (1920). Women couldn't attend boxing matches, though. Effie Fellows, later a world-famous male impersonator, dressed as a boy to sneak into the East Perth bouts in 1900, but was arrested and reprimanded in court.

In 1900, the people voted for WA to join the Commonwealth of Australia the following year. Party politics made its appearance in 1901. The Labour Party took office first in 1904 and again in 1911.

In 1929, King George V declared the City of Perth a 'Lord Mayoralty', amid the celebrations, parades and re-enactments that marked WA's centenary. Fremantle became a city. Loyalty to the Crown was as apparent as

Above: a 1930s view of Barrack Street

ever. All centenary publications carried pictures of King George and Queen Mary. 'Long Live the King' and 'God Bless the Queen' were heard more than any other cries that year. However, suggestion to rename WA 'Kingsland' was turned down.

Centenary euphoria faded with the 1930s Depression, and in 1931, one in four Perth men were jobless. A 5,000-strong protest march ended in fights and arrests. Gold prices improved and many of the unemployed sought work in the goldfields. In 1934, 6 days of race rioting in the gold town of Kalgoorlie – sparked by the bar-fight death of a popular local man – were quelled by armed special police reinforcements from Perth.

As well as the river reclamation work, some building continued, including the Tudor-style London Court and other shopping malls. People with cash could sail to London via Colombo, Bombay and Suez for between £39–104.

Social Customs

Since the colony was born, people had dressed as though they were in Europe, wearing stiff collars, hats and long dresses, with no concessions made to the climate. In the early 20th century, they began to ease their old-world straitjackets. Some people were seen bareheaded in the streets, even with open-neck shirts. Young men wore boaters. (Decades later, hats are back, to ward off skin cancer.)

Isolated City

Perth is the world's most remote capital city, 3,000km (1,864 miles) from the Indonesian capital of Jakarta and almost as far from the nearest Australian capital, Adelaide. Though historical closeness and kinship to the 'old country' has faded, in many ways WA retains its sense of isolation from the rest of the continent, especially the east. This is in part due to physical separation by thousands of kilometres of desert, and part friendly rivalry. 'Wise men from the east' is a caustic comment still heard, and some still talk wistfully of secession! Distances around Perth are still vast but today's instant communications and ease of travel have all but eliminated the remoteness, which persisted even into the 1960s.

Above: evening promenade by the Swan River, circa 1907

In 1869, convicts installed poles for the colony's first electric telegraph line, from Perth to Fremantle. The first link to the outside world came in 1877, via Eucla, to Adelaide, and to London via Overland Telegraph. Perth's telephone service also began in 1887. It was not until 1911 that a submarine cable joined Perth and London.

Swinging Sixties and Onward

Better communications and access to other cultures helped Perth develop new character as the 1960s brought anti-Vietnam war marches to the streets, rock and roll, and anything else young America had to offer. Hip young men became 'bodgies' dancing with their 'widgies' at Perth's hottest teen spot, the Snake Pit at Scarborough.

It was a decade when Perth grabbed a place in the spotlight, hosting the Commonwealth and Empire Games in 1962. In the same year, orbiting astronaut John Glenn dubbed Perth the 'City of Lights' as it gleamed, a beacon surrounded by thousands of miles of darkness. (Four years later the 1875-established Perth Observatory, which had charted 400,000 star positions by 1920, moved away because the same bright city lights compromised its work!)

The last 3 decades of the millennium began with 'the confident 1970s'. Skyscrapers became neighbours of 19th-century structures; fortunes were made in new mineral booms such as nickel; massive industrial and commercial developments and housing demands doubled the number of suburbs.

The 1980s were the decade of Fremantle. In 1983, Perth businessman Alan Bond's yacht, *Australia II*, won the America's Cup off Rhode Island. Some say it was Australia's greatest sporting achievement. In a nation famous for sports success that's doubtful, but the America's Cup victory did bring crucial attention to WA, and specifically the port city, where the Cup was defended (unsuccessfully) in 1987. Fremantle couldn't lose; historic buildings were restored and new businesses and services created in preparation for the huge influx of visitors. Already on the map as home port for round-the-world sailors, visiting yacht racers and cruise liners, Fremantle also grew as a desirable and charismatic place to live.

Today, Perth and WA are still growing, and archaeology has the last word. In 1999, experts returned to WA Museum from outback WA with a slab of 3,500-million-year-old stromatolite fossils – earliest proof of life on earth.

history/culture

HISTORY HIGHLIGHTS

40,000BC (approximately) Aborigines populate all of Australia.

1616 Dutch explorer Dirk Hartog is first European on west coast.

1697 Willen de Vlamingh names Swan River after black swans found there.

1829 On 2 May Captain Fremantle plants Union Jack. In June Captain James Stirling arrives to found the Swan River Colony.

1850 Convicts sent from Great Britain to meet the labour shortage. Before transportation ends (1860) they help build Perth.

1856 Queen Victoria grants Perth its city status.

1870 Representative government granted to the colony.

1871 Compulsory school for children aged 6 to 14.

1877 Telegraph links Perth with London via Adelaide; local telephone service begins 10 years later.

1881 Eastern railway links Perth, Fremantle and Guildford.

1885 Gold found at Halls Creek; first payable goldfield declared next year.

1890 Western Australia (WA) gains Responsible Government. (Sir) John Forrest forms first government.

1893 Paddy Hannan's Kalgoorlie find becomes 'The Golden Mile', and the Gold Rush transforms Perth.

1898 Free Education Bill introduced.

1899 Women get the vote, ahead of Britain, Canada and USA.

1899 Perth Electric Tramway begins to supersede horse transport.

1899 Boer War, and 1,231 WA men go to South Africa; 126 die, one wins the Victoria Cross.

1901 Western Australia joins the empire in genuine grief at death of Queen Victoria. Duke of York visits Perth and names Kings Park.

1901 Western Australia becomes a state of federal Australia.

1902 First 'kinema' opens.

1911 The University of Western Australia opens.

1911 WA adopts compulsory military training; later votes for conscription, and plays major role in World War I Gallipoli campaign.

1917 Trans-Australian Railway links WA to eastern states.

1920s Fremantle is the busiest oil-fuelling port in Australia; the world's first long-distance air service operates from Perth centre.

1929 Amid centenary celebrations of the 1829 founding, George V declares Perth as a 'Lord Mayoralty', and Fremantle becomes a city.

1931 One in four Perth men jobless; a 5,000-strong protest march ends in violence and arrests.

1939 The men and women of Perth serve in World War II; the city prepares for air raids.

1959 First TV service begins.

1962 Perth hosts Commonwealth and Empire Games.

1962 'The City of Lights' – astronaut John Glenn's comment when orbiting over Perth.

1963 New airport opens.

1968 Worst tremors in memory rock Perth, and earthquake destroys Meckering, 130km (81 miles) east.

1971 Concert Hall opens, deemed as important as the Town Hall, which was built in 1870.

1978 The HMAS Stirling naval base is set up as home for Australia's submarine fleet.

1979 State celebrates first 150 years.

1983 *Australia II* wins America's Cup off Rhode Island; 1987 defence puts Fremantle on world map.

1999 World's earliest known life-form, 3,500-million-year-old stromatolites, found in outback and brought to Perth's WA Museum.

Left: sunbathing beauties at Cottesloe Beach

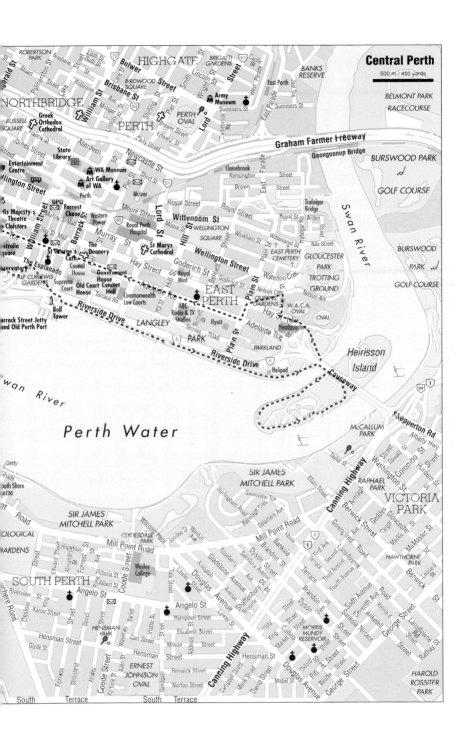

Central Perth

500 m / 450 yards

HIGHGATE

NORTHBRIDGE

PERTH

RUSSELL
SQUARE

Greek Orthodox Cathedral

State Library

WA Museum
Art Gallery of WA

Entertainment Centre

Wellington Street

GPO
Forrest Chase
Western Power

His Majesty's Theatre
The Cloisters

Australia Square

The Esplanade

The Deanery

St George's Cath.

The Conservatory

ALF CURLEWIS GARDENS

Supreme Court

Council House

Government House

Old Court House

Concert Hall

Commonwealth Law Courts

Bell Tower

Barrack Street Jetty and Old Perth Port

Riverside Drive

LANGLEY PARK

Riverside Drive

Helipad

ROBERTSON PARK

Edith St
Brisbane Street
Bulwer Street

BIRDWOOD SQUARE

William Street

PERTH OVAL

Army Museum

BRIGATTI GARDENS

East Perth

Summers St

BANKS RESERVE

Graham Farmer Freeway

Goongoonup Bridge

Claisebrook

Kensington

Brown   Street

Royal Street

Wittenoom St
WELLINGTON SQUARE

Wellington Street

Wickham St

Royal St
Arden

Trafalgar Bridge

Nile Street

Plain Street

EAST PERTH CEMETERY

Goderich St

Royal Mint

Bennett

Goderich St

EAST PERTH

QUEENS GARDENS

ABC Radio & TV Studios

Hyatt

Nelson Cres

Waterloo Cres

GLOUCESTER PARK

TROTTING GROUND

W.A.C.A. OVAL

Police Headquarters

Hay St

Adelaide Tce

PARKLAND

Causeway

Heirisson Island

BELMONT PARK RACECOURSE

BURSWOOD PARK

GOLF COURSE

Swan River

BURSWOOD PARK

GOLF COURSE

McCALLUM PARK

Taylor St

Stepperton Rd

Canning Highway

RAPHAEL PARK

VICTORIA PARK

HAWTHORNE PARK

Berwick

Swan River

Perth Water

SIR JAMES MITCHELL PARK

SIR JAMES MITCHELL PARK

CLYDESDALE PARK

Mill Point Road

Wesley College

SOUTH PERTH

Angelo St

Angelo St

HENSMAN PARK

Hensman Street

Coode Street

Forrest

ERNEST JOHNSON OVAL

South   Terrace

Hurlingham Road

Swanview Tce

Ellam Ave

Mill Point Road

Banksia

Dyson Street

Brandon

Gladstone Avenue

Douglas Avenue

Shaftesbury Avenue

Brandon

Dyson

MORRIS MUNDY RESERVOIR

Hensman St

Canning Highway

Douglas Avenue

George Street

HAROLD ROSSITER PARK

Washington   Colombo St

Berwick Street

George Street

Lansdowne Road

Banksia Terrace

South   Terrace

City Itineraries

1. KINGS PARK AND RIVER WALK *(see map, p18–19)*

A 9am start gives time for a comfortable day that takes in Stirling Gardens, St Georges Terrace and scenic Kings Park, with its panoramic view of the city, Swan River, distant hills and the broad expanse of water that leads the eye towards Fremantle, a vibrant port city. Following a quick tour of the University of Western Australia campus, have lunch, then visit Heirisson Island.

Travel by bus or train to Wellington Street; walk south through Barrack Street to begin this walk where Barrack Street meets St Georges Terrace.

First thing I do with visitors – even en route from the airport, if they're conscious – is show them the stunning city view from Kings Park. So, to get the feel of Perth, use this itinerary.

Start at **Stirling Gardens**, at the corner of Barrack Street and head west along St Georges Terrace. On the north side of the Terrace, note St Martins Tower with the revolving **C Restaurant Lounge** on top. Night or day, it's a grand way to see all of Perth, from the hills to the ocean.

But put the revolving restaurant aside for now, together with the neighbouring mock-Tudor, 1930s-built **London Court**, its St Georges Cathedral and the Dragon clock, and the stylish shopping mall beyond. **Trinity Church** also leads to a shopping arcade, and you can cover all these later (see *Itinerary 3* on page 41).

Exploring St Georges Terrace

The fine old bank building at the corner of William Street was once the **Palace Hotel**, built in sumptuous style in 1895. Habitués still mourn the passing of one of Perth's best pubs, but at least the building was preserved. Its restrained French Second Empire style is in brilliant contrast with the Bankwest Tower which looms above. This was built by Australian businessman Alan Bond at the height of his success and fame, with a penthouse office at the top of the tower to house his multi-million dollar art acquisitions. All along the Terrace you'll trip over such famous names, set in bronze memorial plaques. A total of 150 plaques were installed in 1979 for the 150th anniversary of statehood. Since then, the roll of local heroes has been joined by 10 more, among them round-the-world solo yachtsman Jon Sanders and literary giant Elizabeth Jolley.

Perth Technical School, further on the south side, includes the church-styled 1860s Perth Boys' School. Now carefully preserved, it's the state headquarters of the **National Trust**.

Cross the Terrace where Mill Street comes in from the south to see **The Cloisters**, built by Bishop Hale in 1858 as the colony's first sec-

Left: Government House gardens being dwarfed by highrises
Right: kangaroo sculpture on St Georges Terrace

ondary school for boys. The building is now part of Newman House but Bishop Hale's Church of England Collegiate School moved on. As plain Hale School, located now at Wembley Downs, it's still one of Western Australia's best regarded, and still educates many of the WA influential. A roll call of early pupils – Forrest, Parker, Burt, Wittenoom, Roe – is like scanning a map of state place names. John Forrest, for instance, was an explorer, WA's first state premier, and a pioneer member in the Australian parliament's House of Representatives in Melbourne until he died in 1918. Forrest was also the first Australian member of the UK House of Lords.

The Terrace is now a canyon of new office blocks but fortunately some old buildings are preserved – such as that at 237, on the south side – and used as offices. Behind 235 (the passageway alongside is private property, and officially off limits) is Bishop Hale's own house, built in 1859. With gardens and tennis courts, it makes a startling oasis within the business district. Proper access to **Bishops House** is at the corner of Spring Street and Mounts Bay Road. The verandahs are the sole concession to West Australian sun, wind and rain, tacked on like a skirt around a design that is four-square Georgian. Most early settlers arrived from rural England, and their buildings show an understandable desire to replicate their original homes. (The architect is unknown, but original drawings probably came from a pattern book, with later input from Richard Roach Jewell.)

Anne Neil's modern sculpture, *Going Home*, at the corner of Mount Street, comments on this meeting of cultures. A little brass plaque in the footpath explains what kangaroos with briefcases are doing here.

Kings Park and environs

Where St Georges Terrace veers left up to the park and changes name to Malcolm Street, you'll see the remnants of the **Barracks** gateway on the north side. This was preserved after a public outcry in 1966 when the rest of the Pensioners Barracks was demolished to make way for the Mitchell Freeway. Walk though the arch and the freeway is below you, crowned by the unremarkable grey **Parliament** buildings (tel: 08-9222 7222) and cascading fountains. Visits are possible, especially when parliament is sitting, but call the information office first.

The Barracks, built in 1863–6, is a typical brick-built late-19th-century Perth building which housed the Enrolled Pensioner Force, made up of British soldiers who arrived as convict guards and stayed when army numbers were cut. In 1904, it became the headquarters of the Public Works department, and in the office immediately above this archway, visionary engineer C Y O'Connor planned the revolutionary pipeline concept that would eventually pump water to the goldfields. O'Connor then fought scepticism and opposition to deliver the scheme. Cross the freeway and take it easy up 'heartbreak hill', as it's known to the 15–20,000 runners and walkers who take part in the City to Surf event every winter.

At the Edith Cowan clocktower, turn into Fraser Avenue and **Kings Park** *(see also page 51)*. This approach is a bit like the Charge of the Light Brigade – 'cannons to the left of you, cannons to the right'. The park roads are heavy with military memorabilia and even the ranks of towering lemon-scented gums are a memorial, to mark WA's 1929 centenary. But the main attraction of this walk is less sombre – the view of Perth that's an abiding memory of any Perth visit.

On Fraser Avenue immediately on your left are the first of the cannons, and one of the most colourful memorials. The 'Noble tableaux' at its base depict the heroic exploits of West Australian servicemen in the South African War of 1899–1902. Nearby is a stack of more modern shells, from the battleship *Queen Elizabeth*, making a collection box for visitors to do their bit to support the 'soldiers and sailors' avenues of the park. Small white-on-black plaques before every gum tree on the main roads of May Drive and Lovekin Drive commemorate the fallen warriors.

The new and period buildings at left are some of Perth's most prestigious addresses, and 100m (109yds) on you will see why. Sneak a first glimpse of what you're here for – the spectacular view over the city and river. The view is accessible most of the way from the park entrance, but it's best seen from the Cenotaph war memorial, where there are telescopes, or the lookout above the Aboriginal Heritage Centre.

Before you get there, if you want detailed information about special park

Top left: St Georges Terrace coat-of-arms
Left: Kings Park, the green lung of Perth city. **Above:** lazy Sunday at Kings Park

events and walks, take the short slip road on the right to the park administration building, a low-profile brown-tiled structure; it looks like a roof erupting from the lawns.

Just past this road, and a comfortable old pavilion if you need some restful shade, are more cannons guarding a formidable Queen Victoria. Two of these guns were made in 1843 and used in the Crimea War; the other pair is even older. Made in 1813–4, these cannons may have been used by

Wellington's forces in the decisive Battle of Waterloo which finally crushed Napoleon Bonaparte.

Further on is the award-winning **Frasers Restaurant** (tel: 08-9481 7100), where you can eat at virtually any time and enjoy the river view (Mon–Fri breakfast at 7am, lunch at noon, dinner at 6pm; weekend start times 7.30am, 12.30pm and 6pm). Next door is the park kiosk for snacks and ice cream, and a souvenir kiosk. Many Perth restaurants are BYO (bring your own) for alcohol. Some, like Frasers, are fully licensed but may let you bring your own wine in special circumstances. Generally, expect to pay a corkage charge.

Some visitors might like to take advantage of the vintage-tram-styled vehicles which stop outside Frasers for Kings Park/University of Western Australia or the City of Perth tours. The more energetic ones can find hire bikes near the kiosk. Opposite is **Aboriginal Heritage Centre** (Mon–Fri 10.30am–4pm; Sat–Sun noon–4pm; www.aboriginalgallery.com.au), with the lookout located above. Go down below and check out fine indigenous arts and crafts, and maybe meet the Aboriginal artist in residence. Stay on

the road, rather than the path, to approach the Cenotaph through the **Whispering Wall**, which commemorates major battlefields where Australians fought. The huge river gum just past the Whispering Wall was planted by Queen Elizabeth II in 1954, during one of her many tours of Australia.

Cenotaph

Across the lawns, the **State War Memorial Cenotaph** is WA's principal World War I and II memorial. Set on the edge of Kings Park's escarpment, the illuminated 18-m (59-ft) high obelisk is visible day or night from all around Perth Water, where the Swan River widens into a board bay. Up here you feel on equal terms with city skyscrapers. Thankfully, Perth has made no attempt at world records; it has a conservative approach to high-rise buildings in general. Apart from the central business district (CBD) and some multi-storey apartment blocks you'll see downriver, Perth's only other tall building is the Hotel Rendezvous Observation City at Scarborough Beach.

Ten years ago, a UK television documentary claimed Perth's freeway was a 'road in search of traffic'. Well, the search is over. Beside the small lake below you, a new Narrows Bridge has been built alongside the old to help uncork the rush hour traffic bottleneck. The **Narrows Bridge** and freeway interchange opened in 1959 on land reclaimed from the Swan. Small remnant lakes around the structure are set in surprisingly cool and verdant gardens, and fortunately all survived the building of the extra bridge. If you're fit for a diversion, a staircase (Jacob's Ladder) leads down the escarpment to the lakes. The climb back up can be tough going, though! Clinging to the bank below the CBD buildings are the **Barrack Street Jetty** and **Old Perth Port**, which you'll see up close later on, maybe to make a lunch stop. Ferries from the jetty sail up-river to the valley wineries, down-river 20km (12½ miles) to Fremantle, and across to Rottnest Island. The broad stretch of river at the CBD is **Perth Water**, a busy waterway usually dotted with surfcats, sail boats and ferries. Right of the Narrows Bridge, the river leads to **Melville Water**, a lake-like expanse that is perfect for sailing and fringed by yacht clubs such as the Flying Squadron, Royal Perth and Freshwater Bay Club.

Across the river from the CBD is South Perth, where riverside homes enjoy spectacular 24-hour views of the city. The metropolis, seen at dawn across a mirror-surface river, at sunset with water and multi-coloured sky reflected in glass towers, or illuminated at night, makes living on the south side bearable. In the far distance are the 'Perth Mountains', as older locals scathingly call the modest Darling Ranges. But Australians are notably restrained in their praise of anything.

Top left: hop onto a Kings Park vintage tram if walking is not your thing
Left and above: one for the family album

Botanic Gardens

Walking on from the Cenotaph, you enter
the heavily planted sections of the **Botanic
Gardens**. Remember on this section of the
walk to keep the river on your left. If you
decide to explore any of the paths on the left
or right, return to the main path to continue.

You may well be tempted. There are many
exotic plants, and the gardens are home to
many hundreds of native species. In the
spring wildflower season from August to October, the Western Australian countryside is
a spectacular display of some 10,000 species,
6,000 of them native to the state. This can
surprise first-time visitors who picture Australia as a desert with a beach around the
edge. In spring, many varieties of the kangaroo paw, WA's state plant, flower in the
gardens. This is a strange plant whose flower resembles a paw tipped with
small white 'claws'.

Kings Park is unique. No other city in the world has such a large area of
natural bushland at its heart. The cultivated gardens with lawns, terraces
and water gardens are substantial, but make up only a small part of the 400
hectares (988 acres) of park, which is mainly native bush.

This walk follows mostly paved walkways. For a taste of Australian bush
without leaving the city, consider returning for a half-day bush
or wildflower tour. Call **Visitor Information Centre** (tel:
08-9480 3634; www.bgpa.wa.gov.au; daily 9.30am–4pm) for
details of guided walks. Past the memorials is a small rotunda,
the first building along the path. Divert right to the Pioneer
Women's Memorial Fountain and lake. A stream and richly
inlaid path leads down to the Women's Suffrage Pavilion (another cool resting place.) Return to the riverside
walkway, and the building glimpsed through the trees
is the **Old Swan Brewery**. Restored after years of controversy – some claim this site is sacred, home of a
mysterious creature called the Wagyl – it's likely to
become a complex of shops, restaurants and apartments. Depending on time of day there could be
countless yachts on this stretch of river. The far shore
is a para-sailing and water-ski area.

Native bush plants edge the path all the way, olive and
sage green rather than the lusher northern hemisphere emer-
alds. Some of the most distinctive are the banksias, zamias
and grass trees, also known as 'the coconut of the south west'
because of the many uses Aborigines make of them. Fire stim-
ulates growth and blackens the fire-resistant trunk, also giving
them the common name of 'blackboy'.

Above: kangaroo's paw, WA's state plant
Right: sculpture at University of Western Australia

A set of steps by a small steel barrier on the left leads down to the river road. Don't take them unless you enjoy climbing up and down stairs. Instead, follow the right fork. At the end, turn left into Park Avenue. This is one of the best addresses in a city where most neighbourhoods have their merits. Apart from the facilities available in these Park Avenue towers – gymnasia, pools, tennis courts and underground garages – the combination of uncluttered views across the river and city, with Kings Park as a bush backyard, makes apartment living here special.

University tour

Administration buildings and residential colleges of the UWA (University of Western Australia; www.uwa.edu.au) line the avenue all the way to Winthrop Avenue. Of these, **St George's College**, whose crenellated towers and flag pole can be seen, is the most picturesque.

Turn left at Winthrop Avenue and follow the footpath through a short subway under Stirling Highway, called Mounts Bay Road, into the university – and back 70 years ago. The classic mediterranean styling of the first UWA buildings is much older, of course, but in the 1930s the university began to move from the corrugated steel sheds in Perth, where it began teaching in 1913. UWA was the British Commonwealth's first free university.

Across the Reflecting Pool is **Winthrop Hall**, with its undercroft terracotta frieze of gryphons and 50-m (164-ft) clocktower; to your right, across **Whitfield Court**, the colonnaded building is the original library, now the administration block; more pillars hold up **Hackett Hall**, on your left.

All were built with an endowment from Sir John Winthrop Hackett, and established the UWA at Crawley in 1932. Hackett was the first chancellor of the UWA, and also owner of Perth's daily newspaper, the *West Australian*. Designs were by Victorian architects Sayce and Alsop, who won an international competition for the commission.

Cross the lawn alongside the pool, turn left and walk through the **Great Gateway**. Architecturally it refers to the pyloned gateways of Egypt, as well as the Tudor ones of Oxford and Cambridge. Above is the **Senate Room**, where the university's governors meet, watched over by the *Five Lamps of Learning*, a Venetian glass tile mosaic by Victorian artist Walter Napier.

Through the arch, turn right to reach the **Sunken Garden**, a secluded retreat and a cool, shady place to sit and take stock. You might

Right: UWA was designed by Victorian architects Sayce and Alsop

decide to spend a couple of hours on the campus, where heritage-listed gardens, thousands of native trees, art works and architecture combine harmoniously. The **Visitors' Centre** at the north end of the administration building sells a very inexpensive but comprehensive booklet, and also gives out free pamphlets on campus art works, concerts, theatre productions and guided tours.

The Sunken Garden is an amphitheatre that can seat 350 people. The first performance in 1948 was of *Oedipus Rex*, and it's still used for Festival of Perth productions. Curved stone benches around the sundial carry the following inscription, which recounts the prayer of Ru, a Maori leader separated from his migrating tribe by a storm:

Tangaroa Clear Away the Clouds
That Ru May see the Stars

Walk back to Winthrop Hall, and unless you plan to explore the campus, take Saw Promenade towards Reid Library, turn left at the Arts building and cross Hackett Drive to the river. During semester, you could have coffee and a snack at Hackett Hall or in its courtyard; alternatively, there's the refectory, another café below the library, or even the Tavern if you want to see undergrads working hard at their social studies. Some 200m (220 yds) downstream, turning right when you reach the riverbank, are **Matilda Bay Tea Rooms**, and then **Matilda Bay Seafood Restaurant**. Both are good lunch stops. At the café, you may have to fight off seagulls who want their share. The restaurant is more sedate, if expensive.

By the river

Students use the riverbank as a hangout to study, have lunch, or just chat. If you see any of them leap into the Swan fully dressed, don't panic. They will be first-year students naive enough to have gambled on their table-football talent in the Tavern. A dive into the river is the penalty for losing 7–0. You're more likely to see kids kayaking off the jetty or playing on the riverside sand. The view across the water, past the craft moored at the Royal Perth Yacht Club, is of the city and the mound of Kings Park, which you have just walked.

To return to town, walk back upriver, keeping the water on the right, past the old boathouse of the Perth Dinghy Sailing Club. Cross the main Mounts Bay Road at the end of Hackett Drive and take the bus from the front of St George's College for a 5-minute journey to the new busport back in town.

At the busport, head for **Old Perth Port**. Follow the walk signs for William Street, cross William into the Esplanade lawns and if it's cool, duck into the glass pyramid. It's a conservatory of tropical plants, with welcome humidity in winter. The jetty is across the lawns at the junction of Barrack and Riverside Drive. Dominating the jetty is the spectacular **Swan Bells** (more popularly known as the bell tower by locals) with its sail-shaped copper

Above: the futuristic Swan Bells
Right: Matilda Bay

wings housing a gift to the city – the bells from St Martin's-in-the-Field, Trafalgar Square, London. All the cruise and ferry operators are here, plus the Transperth 'Zoo' ferry. Transperth is Perth's public transportation system. You can book all river and Rottnest trips, as well as lunch and dinner cruises, or rent self-drive launches for up to 10 people. All the cruise companies keep to the Swan, and self-hire is a good alternative if you like exploring. Cruising downriver in a smaller craft you can follow the Canning River instead. Simply keep to the south bank, and sail under the Canning Bridge.

There are good places to pull in for food and drinks, too, such as **Raffles Hotel** at Canning Bridge. If you stay on the Swan, **Point Walter** on the south bank, en route to Fremantle, has an excellent licensed café – but watch out for the sandbar stretching halfway across the Swan.

More lunch options

Lunch may be the main consideration right now, and there's a good choice from **Shun Fung** Chinese seafood restaurant; **Moorings**, licensed and open from breakfast to dinner, serving 'native' foods such as emu and kangaroo; **Barnacles** snack bar; and **Lucky Shag** bar (open daily, from noon till late). This is a small pub overlooking the river, with a good range of beers and wine.

Right next to the Old Perth Port is the restored clapboard boathouse of **Western Australia Rowing Club**. You could have after-lunch coffee here. The club was founded in 1868 and its boathouse, which was built in 1905, is now National Trust-listed.

After lunch, stroll east along Riverside Drive to **Heirisson Island**. Hundreds of palms fringe the road and landscaped gardens and most of the traffic is due to disappear when Riverside Drive goes underground.

The green expanse separating the city and Swan River is Langley Park, Perth's first airfield. The park is used regularly for special events, and echoes annually to the howl of Rally Australia cars. Occasionally, small aircraft still fly in. Helicopter trips are operated here too, by **Preston Helicopters** (tel: 08-9414 1000; www.prestonheli.com.au).

Heirisson Island

The walk to Heirisson Island can be done comfortably in 30 minutes. Just before the causeway to Heirisson, check out **About Bike Hire** (tel: 08-9221 2665; www.aboutbikehire.com.au; daily 10am–5pm; Sun 10am–4pm) for bikes, tandems, family four-seaters, kayaks and in-line skates.

Reach the island by following the path up onto the causeway. The first rickety causeway spanned the Swan in 1843, and as late as the 1950s some desperate unemployed made camps on Heirisson Island. Today, the most important residents are kangaroos. As you cross the causeway, look right, for a bright orange sign on the island. Turn right off the bridge, follow the track down onto the island and walk towards the sign, with the river on your right. Check the sign before entering the kangaroo sanctuary as these are wild animals. Don't go too close. During the heat of the day kangaroos stay under cover, but if you move quietly around the track, there's a good chance of finding them grazing. Rangers feed them between 7–8am and 3–4pm. Following the perimeter track near the tip of the island, watch for the bronze statue of Yagan. A warrior leader of Aborigines, Yagan was killed in 1833, in a conflict with the white newcomers. The island is a lovely place to picnic – wait for the day to cool, the kangaroos to emerge and the setting sun to reflect back at you from the city's glass towers. Bring takeaway food and drinks from the Old Port and finish the day here.

When you're ready to leave, stay on track and exit at the far gates, then with the enclosure on your left, return to the causeway and retrace your steps. Go down and follow the path which passes under the causeway, follow it approximately 150m (163yds) towards the light towers of the **WACA** (Western Australian Cricket Association), and exit the parkland at Trinity Avenue. Cross Trinity and walk along a noisy stretch of busy Hay Street, which leads to the tranquil **Queens Gardens**.

Top: cricket match at the WACA
Left: Peter Pan statue at Queens Gardens

You could also take a look inside the WACA (if you want to sound like a local, pronounce it 'Wacker'). If you're lucky, a day/night cricket match will be on. Even non-sports fans find the spectacle of cricket played under the lights in multi-coloured uniforms fascinating, and the ground is worth seeing anyway. West Australians are justifiably proud of their cricket head-quarters, and the State team which has produced dozens of internationals, and world beaters such as Dennis Lillee. Australia's domestic interstate cricket competition, the Sheffield Shield (now renamed PURA Cup), began in 1892. Though WA only joined the contest in 1949, the team has taken the Shield 15 times since. Other sports are played at the WACA, including in recent years baseball, Australian Rules football and gaelic football. Massive redevelopment in 2002 improved all spectator facilities while preserving a 'traditional' cricket ground ambience. Call the WACA (tel: 08-9265 7222; www.waca.com.au) to check on match fixtures.

Enter Queens Gardens at the corner of Hale Street and Nelson Crescent. **Queens Gardens** is one of Perth's earliest, and its lake was originally claypits that provided bricks for many early buildings. There are lily ponds, English trees and, most impressive of all, a replica made in 1927 of Sir George Frampton's statue of Peter Pan. The original of J M Barrie's immortal boy who never grew up is in London's Kensington Gardens. This copy, autographed by Barrie, was bought in 1928 by the Rotary Club of Perth as a gift to the children of WA.

Leave Queens Gardens at the far corner, at the junction of Hay and Plain streets, and walk south towards the river for Adelaide Terrace. Turn right at the Hyatt Hotel, which faces the historic **Anglican Girls Orphanage**, now a National Trust building housing the Heritage Council. Parts of this road, which transforms into St Georges Terrace at Victoria Avenue, are set for redevelopment, but the south side becomes a parade of high-quality hotels. **The Duxton**, at No 1 St Georges Terrace, has an unusual recent history. Until redeveloped in 1996, it was the Perth tax office. Opinion was divided between those who thought it the biggest egg-box in the state, and others who said such fine 1960s architecture must be

preserved. Preservers won, the taxmen shifted, and now the Duxton is one of Perth's finest. Next door is **Perth Concert Hall**. No controversy about this – historian Dr Tom Stannage says that its creation in 1971 was as important for the spirit and self-confidence of the city as Perth Town Hall was in 1860. It is a superb auditorium.

The walk ends at Stirling Gardens where you began, close by the 1960s **Council House** and kangaroo sculptures on the footpath. There's a thought: in a single day you could see the real live ones on Heirisson island, their over-size images on the Terrace, and then eat them for dinner at Old Perth Port.

Above: Heirisson island is home to a kangaroo sanctuary

2. HISTORIC BUILDINGS AND THE MINT *(see map, p33)*

This walk traces Perth's past through pre- and post-boom historic buildings. At the Perth Mint you may hold, admire, savour, even invest in some of the stuff that made Perth rich – gold.

Take the bus or train to Wellington Street; walk south through Barrack Street to begin this walk where Barrack Street meets St Georges Terrace.

Gold transformed Western Australia in the 1890s and financed a building boom in its revitalised capital city. Surrounded by towers of steel and glass, 19th-century buildings are now sturdy yet genteel neighbours of the 'here today, gone tomorrow' commercial shopfronts. The earliest of the historic buildings recall times before the streets were paved with gold, or even tarmac. Many more followed the 1890s boom.

The Deanery, at the corner of Pier Street and St Georges Terrace, is a good spot to pick up the trail of old Perth. You are standing in the earliest street, close to the site where first settlers pitched their tents. On the south side of St Georges Terrace are Stirling Gardens and Perth's first brick structure, the old **Court House**. Next door is **Government House**, residence of the state's governor. All around you is the traffic and bustle of the business centre of Perth.

Ecclesiastical Buildings

The Deanery was built in 1859 by Matthew Blagden Hale, first Bishop of Perth and one of its most influential characters. Bishops House and The Cloisters are among his best-known buildings, and Hale School is perhaps the state's most prestigious (see *Itinerary 1*).

Hale first came to Perth in 1856, some 6 years after the labour-starved colony began shipping in convicts. He was strongly opposed to penal colonies – 'Convictions yes, convicts no' could have been his personal motto, and he backed his beliefs when investing personal wealth into city buildings. However, by the time work began at The Deanery non-convict builders were scarce, and the good bishop was forced to employ paroled prisoners, or 'ticket-of-leavers'.

Hale overcame his principles by opining that these felons would achieve moral reformation through daily contact with God-fearing men such as himself and the man in need of a roof over his head, Dean Pownall. Ticket-of-leavers had something to gain too. After working their parole for up to 4 years they could achieve a conditional pardon.

Above: historic Government House
Left: traffic stopper

A little further west along St Georges Terrace is another ecclesiastical encounter. Had **St Georges Cathedral** (daily 7am–5pm) been built a decade later, you would see a much grander building. But it was started in 1879 when times were hard, and work ended in 1888, with the WA gold rush still 4 years off. They couldn't even afford a spire.

The cathedral's architect was Edmund Blackett, whose Great Hall at Sydney University is said to be one of Australia's best buildings. Look inside, where jarrah-framed ceiling and stained glass complement the bricks and limestone that Blackett used to summon the medieval period. The Gothic revivalist architect never travelled west to Perth to see his plans take shape; one wonders how he would have reacted to the square tower added in 1902, as yet another of the empire's countless memorials to Queen Victoria.

The **Central Government Offices**, next door and almost a whole block long, took more than 30 years to finish in the Second Empire Parisian style. WA's first Roman Catholic governor, Frederick Weld, began the project with a Treasury building in 1874. By 1905, the General Post Office and other government departments had been added. Fashion was then reaching out to Perth – this opulent style reflects that used by architect Baron Haussmannin in remodelling Paris, and copied worldwide during Napoleon III's Second Empire (1850–70).

city itineraries

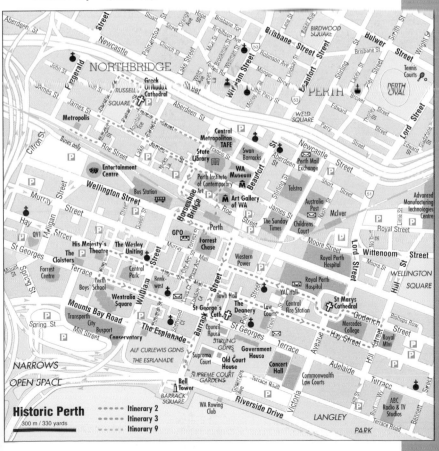

Historic Perth

300 m / 330 yards

- - - Itinerary 2
- - - Itinerary 3
- - - Itinerary 9

Gold Rush Era Architecture

Turn right into Barrack Street to see what the gold strike of 1892 did for Perth, when commercial buildings boomed and architects flocked to Perth. Keep your head up, though, because most of their early work has been eradicated at street level. Crowning the surf shops, ice cream parlours and travel agents, some turn-of-the-19th century upper facades survive. Three of these, including the former **McNess Royal Arcade** of 1897, rise above their mundane roots on the west side of Barrack Street.

There are more superior 'uppers' later, some in Barrack Street, but now turn right into Hay Street at the corner of **Perth Town Hall** (1867–70). Now hemmed in by surrounding developments, the Town Hall's impor-

tance to those early residents is hard to imagine. But early photographs show it clear and unencumbered, its clocktower visible for miles. It was a sign that Perth was going to last, and very handy for the majority of people who had no watches.

The Town Hall is another convict-era building, one of the finest examples of the state's red-brick heritage. Local materials predominate – tough jarrah timbers, Swan Valley limestone and clay bricks from the quarry that later became Queens Gardens. Even local sheoak roof shingles were originally used. (You'll see them if you visit **WA Museum's Old Gaol** on the *Itinerary 3*.) Had it not been 'improved' out of existence, you might now be browsing market stalls below the Town Hall. Copying late-medieval European market squares, the hall's Gothic arched undercroft originally housed a local produce market.

In the 1890s, the fire brigade was stationed under the Town Hall. Firemen borrowed horses from the cabbies in Barrack Street whenever they were called to put out a blaze. Later they had their own animals, trained to trot out of the stables at the sound of the fire bell and wait in front of the hose reels, to be harnessed.

Across Hay Street more period facades face the Town Hall at first floor level, and a little further on is some fine and rare art deco at the **Criterion Hotel**. Next to the Town Hall on the corner of Cathedral Avenue is the 1897 **Titles Office**, thought to be the best example of George Temple Poole's work. Poole was colonial architect and superintendent of public works in the gold rush days. The government scrambled to meet the demands of an increasing population and Poole's office designed 300 public buildings from 1895 to 1897. The Titles Office features many classical devices, such as main columns with Corinthian capitals and others with Ionic or Doric tops. Sweeping entrance archways were a favourite of Poole's; see them at the Perth Mint, too.

Now divert left at the next junction, Pier Street, to see the excellent up-

Above: stylish period 'upper' of former Salvation Army building in Pier Street
Right: making money since 1899, the Perth Mint

pers of buildings, notably the old **Salvation Army** building and **Milton Chambers**. If you make a late start, you could do so from the restaurant at **Sebel Hotel** which is directly opposite, and very good value with its moderately priced set lunch, or à la carte menu.

Pier Street was the Salvation Army's first Perth citadel, designed by Edward Saunders, one of its officers. In 1899, the site and building cost around £8,000. Adjacent buildings were bought and the Army spread around the corner into Murray Street, where you will later see the heritage-listed **Congress Hall**. This was recently converted into stylish inner-city apartments after the Salvation Army built new premises in Perth.

Back on Hay Street, next to Black Swan café is the free-standing front porch of Perth's first purpose-built theatre, **St Georges Hall**. Another 1980s property boom victim that was torn down in 1986, it first opened in 1879 with a performance of *The Colleen Bawn*, by Boucicault.

Walking on, the Fire and Emergency Services monolith looms on the left; if you hear bells and sirens, look out for flying fire engines. Hold this concrete slab in the short-term memory bank; later, compare it with the delightful 1900s-built **Central Fire Station** on Murray Street, where the style screams out louder than fire alarms. The final stylish buildings of Hay Street are next on the left – the **Catholic Church Office** and **Cathedral Presbytery**, facing the art deco façade of **Campbell House**.

After you cross Victoria Avenue, nothing but an uninteresting brick wall seals off Mercedes College. Better views of the campus are to be had in **Victoria Square**, but stay on Hay Street for the direct route to **Perth Mint** (www.perthmint.com.au; Mon–Fri 9am–4pm; Sat–Sun 9am–1pm), just a block away at the junction with Hill Street.

Making Money

Perth Mint began in 1899 as a branch of the Royal Mint, London, and has the look of a tastefully walled and fenced colonial mansion, with two wings, central riser and flag pole. The elegant front lawns feature a statue of prospec-

tors – cast in bronze, presumably, not gold. The glittering stuff is all inside, where you can experience a reconstructed turn-of-the-19th-century miners camp, as well as get your hands on a chunky 400-ounce gold bar. You can also watch a gold pour, held every hour in the original Melting House (Mon–Fri 10am–3pm, Sat–Sun 10am–noon). Your best bet is to be there in time for the heritage walk conducted every half hour (Mon–Fri 9.30am–2.30pm, Sat–Sun 9.30–11.30am), which takes you through the gold exhibition and finishes in time to see the molten gold poured into ingots.

Australia's oldest operating mint was extra busy in the run-up to its 1999 centenary, producing special goods to mark the 2000 Olympic Games in Sydney. There's also a special gold sovereign that replicates the original 1899 version. Souvenirs for sale range from the inexpensive, through moderate and up to sets of nuggets and coins at well over A$1,000. If you intend investing, remember your passport and ticket. International travellers can make tax-free purchases.

A Variety of Victuals

After Perth Mint you might be ready for lunch. If you love seafood, some of the best in town is at the Sheraton Hotel (tel: 08-9224 7777) on nearby Adelaide Terrace. The **Monterey Brasserie** lunch buffet (Mon–Sat noon–2.30pm; Sun 12.30–2.30pm) features endless fresh and smoked fish and crustaceans. Opposite the Mint you'll find more fish among **Wasabi's** Japanese takeaways (tel: 08-9225 6868; Mon–Fri 10.30am–2.30pm; 5–7pm). Inexpensive, and tables are usually available.

There's also the **Grosvenor** pub, now looking very good with its Chill Out café and small garden, and belying the 'grotty Grosvenor' tag of earlier decades. Only the determinedly untouched ceiling of the back bar, where aspiring and established musicians have played for years, looks the way it

used to. Notice the dangling display of compact discs. Local bands tend to launch their new releases with Grosvenor concerts, and top bands perform in the adjacent Chill Room. Lunch at the Chill Out is moderately priced, and if you don't enjoy the smell of beer, eat in the front garden.

After lunch, go north on Hill Street and take the first left turn on Goderich Street into **Victoria Square**, which is dominated by **St Mary's Cathedral** (tel: 08-9223 1351; open daily from 7am). Facing it on your left is **Mercy Convent**, designed by an Irish political prisoner called McMahon and built in 1873. This was base for six Sisters of Mercy who came from Ireland in 1846 and established schools like **Mercedes College**, which is open to students of all denominations. Three distinctive gables with decorative brickwork are original; the iron lacework and verandah were later additions to the convent. With its cathedral, Presbytery and Church Office, which you passed on Hay Street, Victoria Square has been the headquarters of the Roman Catholic faith in Perth since Governor Weld's time.

St Mary's Cathedral is probably based on a design by Pugin, another Gothic revivalist, who co-designed Britain's Houses of Parliament. Pugin died in 1852 and if St Mary's was his work, the drawings were probably brought from London a year later by Perth's Roman Catholic Bishop Serra. Building took 2 years, from 1863–5. Many of the spiky Gothic features were later additions, together with the present spire.

Walking into Victoria Square after the Perth Mint, the 1920s eastern extension confronts you. The grand plan was for this style to eventually cloak the entire structure, but the 1930s Great Depression quashed that. Make sure to see the western side.

Civic Buildings

Leave the square on Murray Street, shadowed by the magnificent Morton Bay fig tree whose canopy spans the road. Many of the buildings along here are now part of the Royal Perth Hospital precinct, but on the left is the aforementioned Central Fire Station (circa 1900), now a **Safety Education Centre and Museum** (tel: 08-9323 9353; Mon–Fri 10am–noon; 1–3pm, closed weekends and holidays). It's worth a look for the old fire Dennis engines alone, still licensed and ready to roll; and there's a 16-man fire appliance which arrived in Fremantle from manufacturer Shand Mason back in 1856.

The front elevation poses the question: did the fire brigade quit the sublime for the ridiculous when it moved here from the Town Hall? Architect Michael Cavanagh threw practically every device into this building: built of rusticated limestone and with arches, like the Perth Mint it is essentially romanesque, but more 'fanciful'. Turreted gables, friezes, spires, iron lace, terracotta chimney pots, covered balconies and pillars – there are even bright red fireman's helmets. Cavanagh had a lot more fun than he did on St Mary's east side.

A parade of historic buildings follows, street to roof structures rather

Top left: time for lunch. **Left:** the former Central Fire Station is now the Safety Education Centre & Museum. **Above:** building detail, Safety Education Centre

than just upper facades, which is all that's left further down the street. On the left there's the **Young Australia League**, next to the heritage-listed **Living Stone Foundation**, followed by the Salvation Army Building and **Congress Hall**. Across the road is the former **Government Printing Office** (1891–4), next door to the **Government Stores** (1911). The Printing Office is interesting, starting calmly at street level and becoming progressively more daring as it rises to the sky, with turrets and domes. It's more of Temple Poole's monumental output. For proof of his versatility, see also the 'Chicago School'-styled **Sheffield House** in Hay Street, built after he left the government and set up his private practice.

The next part of Murray Street, until it crosses Barrack Street and becomes a mall, is mostly new, but again check the uppers. Note Miss Maud's Swiss hotel on the left and several facades above shops on the right. Turn right at Barrack Street to see how heritage has at best been ignored, and sometimes destroyed. On your right find the remnants of **The Railway Hotel**, and opposite, the sadly faded **Seeligson Loan Office**. The pub here opened in 1906 and was known as McCarthy's and by other names until it became The Railway around 1920. It was closed in 1991 and almost completely demolished in 1992. The city council got wind of it and the cavalry charged in, stopping the destruction before the front fell. Phineas Seeligson's pawnbroking business pre-dates the golden years, which is probably why it was always a fancy front only, with totally unadorned sides. Now drab and neglected, it's made even worse by the ugly vertical sign added much later, and now disused.

Walk back up Barrack Street to reach **Hay Street Mall**, but first check out the stonework above Hungry Jacks. This was once **Albany Bell Tea Rooms** (1896), part of a chain run by Mr Albany Bell, who also found dubious fame by introducing ice-cream sundaes and soda fountains to Perth and the Goldfields. The upper facade has classical pilasters and arched win-

Above: Horseshoe Bridge, William Street

dows, and the keystones of each window feature a moustached man, possibly Albany Bell. Thanks to the fast food shop below, perhaps he lives on.

There are numerous places to stop, shop and refresh in the Mall, but press on to William Street and the **Wesley Church** (1867–70). Dwarfed now by skyscrapers, the spire once rivalled the Town Hall clock as an outstanding landmark. Across William Street, continue on Hay Street. Immediately on the left is **E Cucina** café, its shady garden a bonus provided by the new tower blocks. Other cafés follow, all of them good, such as **CBD**, which has an enterprising menu, including the reasonably-priced 'stack of tastes', a three-in-one dish for two people, wine included. Remember this as an option for dinner – followed perhaps by a show at His Majesty's Theatre *(see below)*.

If you take an afternoon break at the CBD, sit and consider the art deco 'factory' design of the **Harpers Building** against the surrounding upper facades of a much earlier era – such as the immediately adjacent A W Dobbie, built in 1861, above Boffins bookshop. An alternative is the quirkily named **44 King Street**, which has great coffee and home-made bread. It's at (surprise, surprise) 44 King Street (turn right at His Majesty's Theatre and go north), in one of many stylish buildings restored as part of the inner city regeneration. Across the street from 44 is the Greenhill Gallery, well worth a look to see current West Australian artists' work.

An Evening at the Theatre

But the building you're here to see is **His Majesty's Theatre**, a symbol of Perth's established prosperity when built in 1904 for £42,000 by entrepreneur, mayor and parliamentarian Thomas Molloy. He made his fortune from hotels and theatres and 'His Maj' was the greatest of them all, seating 2,584 patrons on three levels around a horseshoe-shaped auditorium. It opened on Christmas Eve with an 'extravaganza', *The Forty Thieves*.

An extravagant feature lost with restoration (and the advent of air-conditioning) was the dome, which winched open on hot Perth nights for expansive views of the night sky.

Millions of government dollars were spent to restore the theatre in the 1970s, with much of architect William Wolf's splendid wedding-cake exterior preserved.

After the theatre, go south along King Street and turn left at St Georges Terrace. Walk past Trinity Church and old Palace Hotel and cross the Terrace to go south towards the river down Howard Street. This street was created in 1897 as a Terrace/river link and became a legal profession enclave, rich in Edwardian and Victorian buildings. Some remain, such as **20 Howard Street** (1905). Made of Donnybrook stone

Left: His Majesty's Theatre boasts a grand horseshoe-shaped auditorium

in Gothic revival style, No 20 was created by a respected architect Charles Oldham. The metal grill over the front door bears the initials of his clients, law firm Haynes, Robinson and Cox.

Turn left at the bottom of the hill and walk east on the Esplanade. At the corner of Barrack Street is the **Weld Club**, built in 1892 by Talbot Hobbs and named after Governor Weld. Equivalent to the London 'gentlemen's clubs', the Weld was exclusive to the rich and mighty. A predominant feature is the belvedere corner tower, which would have commanded wonderful views across the Swan before much of it was reclaimed. The Weld was, and still

is, Perth's most influential club. In this age of equal rights and opportunities, enquiries about membership policy are met with a polite 'no comment' by the club secretary.

Just across Barrack Street, enter lush **Stirling Gardens** for the **Supreme Court of WA** (1903) and the old **Court House** (1836). Some public parts of the Supreme Court are accessible and you can sit in on trials, mostly timed between 10am–1pm and 2.15–4.15pm. Serious criminal and civil cases are tried here. Check with the entrance hall staff what cases are proceeding, and they'll also advise you on behaviour in court.

The old Court House is a fitting finale to this historical tour. Perth's oldest building, it sits where the first settlers' tents were pitched in August 1829. Crime was rare then and the Court House was used for a variety of purposes, including worship, entertainment and education. For a simple building, it gained a fair share of folklore. A piano concert given here in 1846 by Father Dom Salvado raised money for the monks to finance their mission and bring Christian care to the Aborigines north of Perth. The performance united Anglican, Jewish and Catholic people to the cause and led to the establishment of the Benedictine monastery at New Norcia (see *Excursion 2*). The downside for Perth society was the loss of such a fine musician to the Bush.

Court House architect Henry Reveley would not have grown famous for his design, but he didn't need to. History will remember him as the man who saved poet Percy Shelley from drowning in the Arno in 1818. Reveley went on to design the first **Government House** (1834–8). Shelley went on to drown in the Mediterranean. Before Reveley's Government House was finished, Governor Stirling sat writing dispatches under an umbrella in a leaky 1829 hut. The present building was completed in 1863, but Reveley's also stood in the grounds until the 1890s, when the gardens were extended and a large ballroom built.

In 1925, one of Perth's most notorious events took place in this ballroom. After dance No 13, a beautiful young woman walked to the centre of the floor, produced a pistol and shot dead her erstwhile boyfriend. After a sensational trial she was acquitted and vanished, never to be seen again in Perth.

Above: Government House dates back to 1863

3. CULTURE AND SHOPPING *(see map, p33)*

Perth's major galleries and museums can easily absorb you all day. For inveterate shoppers, however, the shopping options at Forrest Chase may be a stronger draw. Round the day off with dinner at a revolving restaurant offering a bird's-eye view of Perth.

Travel by bus or train to Wellington Street station, and walk to Forrest Chase. The suggested highlights can be seen in a morning, but visitors with strong cultural interests can linger in the museums and still make time for shopping. Remember that some of the smaller shops close earlier on Saturday.

Start at Forrest Chase, the hub of the shopping area. It's a lively place all day, with buskers and other entertainment, and good for a snack meal outside. Take the upper walkway to cross Wellington Street, go through the station concourse and on to the cultural centre. Walk by the Art Gallery of Western Australia *(see page 43)*, which you will return to later, and head past the startling artwork, *The Caller* by Gerhard Marks, and the pool to the **State Library** (Mon–Thurs 9am–8pm, Fri 9am–5.30pm, Sat–Sun 10am–5.30pm).

Given enough research time all you need to know about Perth can be found in this reference library containing state archives, film and photographs. The main attraction for visitors, though, is likely to be the discard book shop in the front lobby, where real bargains cost as little as A$1.

From the library cross the concourse to **PICA**, the Perth Institute of Contemporary Art (www.pica.org.au; tel: 08-9227 6144; exhibitions Tues–Sun 11am–7pm). The 1896 red-brick building was a school until the 1980s, and is now a hub of avant-garde arts action. The main gallery is a soaring room that was the main school hall; the original classrooms on the mezzanine are now all studios. A small theatre is at the ground level. Friendly people run the front desk; ask them about all performances. You can also pick up a copy

Above: multi-cultural arts scene
Right: *The Caller*, a sculpture by Gerhard Marks

of *Arts and Cultural Guide* for Perth and Fremantle, with information on small galleries and attractions.

Also part of PICA is the nearby **Arts House**, with the **Photographers Gallery**, **Western Australia Actors Centre** and **Impressions Gallery**, which shows local prints. Performances at the Actors Centre are advertised on the spot. Entry to PICA exhibitions is usually free; donations are accepted.

Ancient Life Forms

Walk back past the library towards Beaufort Street for the entrance to the **Western Australian Museum** (tel: 08-9427 2700; www.museum.wa.gov.au; daily 9.30am–5pm, free entry). Pick up a free gallery plan at the front desk.

In 1999, the earliest evidence of life on earth was discovered in the Western Australian Pilbara region – and you can see it here in the **Dinosaur Gallery** in the Jubilee Building. Among the bones and footprints, this prize exhibit looks like nothing more than a slab of red rock. But it is the oldest life fossil known, stromatolites estimated to be 3,500 million years old. Coniform stromatolites are made when limestone sediments are trapped by algae and take millions of years to form. Live versions are still growing in the highly saline water of Hamelin Pool at Shark Bay in the north of WA.

Australia began taking on its present-day form 120 million years ago when the supercontinent Gondwana began to break up, separating South America, Africa, Madagascar and India from Australia. South America was connected to Australia at its southern tip, via an ice-free Antarctica, until 30 million years ago. Isolated since then, Australia's prehistoric life forms were unthreatened by man until perhaps 40,000–50,000BC, and botanists believe Australia was the prime location of early flowering plant evolution.

Some of the weird and wonderful creations of isolation survive – such as the duck-billed platypus, kangaroo and wallaby. The **Jubilee Building** has them, nevertheless in glass cases, with many less well-known species such as the mulgara and wombat, and threatened species like the quokka and noisy scrub bird.

Above: intriguing 1917 pharmacy in the Old Goal museum

Sadly, for some like the Tasmanian tiger it's too late. Although farmers on Australia's southerly island claim to see them – always in the distance – and scientists talk of cloning from bottled remains, the only one you're likely to see is here. It was really a marsupial, not a cat – proper name thylacine, or Tasmanian wolf. The stripes gave it a bad name.

Another oddity is an egg of the Elephant Bird. No joke, this gigantic beast became extinct in Madagascar 300–400 years ago. Its egg is bigger than a football, good for 70 omelettes when early Madagascans threw a big family brunch. The museum's fossilised egg was uncovered in sand dunes near Cervantes, north of Perth, and had probably floated across the Indian Ocean.

Exiting the Jubilee Building, go into the Beaufort Courtyard, where there's a pleasant coffee shop and the **Old Gaol**. Built by convicts in 1855–6, it was both gaol and courthouse until 1889. Before the Jubilee Building opened 10 years later, this was also the museum, started with a geological collection assembled by the chaplain of Fremantle prison.

Externally restored, the Old Gaol is now crammed with memorabilia of Perth life since Stirling's expedition of 1827. There's a photograph of Governor Hampton presenting commissions to Volunteer Force officers in 1863; the complete original courtroom; a pedal radio used by outback families; a complete 1917 pharmacy; and clothes, toys and furniture. Nervous visitors should avoid the 1970s dental surgery, which looks frighteningly Victorian.

If time allows, look into the Francis Street natural history wing – it's worth it if only to see how termites build their own skyscrapers. This one is just 2m (6½ft) high; they can reach 7m (23ft).

Australian Art

Next, step into the **Art Gallery of Western Australia** (tel: 08-9492 6600; www.artgallery.wa.gov.au; daily 10am–5pm), where more than 1,000 treasured works of art are displayed, including an aboriginal art collection that is possibly the best in Australia; and Australian and international paintings, sculpture, prints, crafts and decorative arts. Special and touring exhibitions are mounted every year and it's worth a call to find out what's current. You might want to allow more time, but entry delays are unlikely even for the most popular shows.

Major works are regularly rotated to make best use of space, but a must-see is the **Centenary Gallery** – featuring some truly great Australian works such as *Down on his Luck*, Fred McCubbin; *Breaking the News*, John Longstaff; *Black Thursday*, William Strutt; *Ada Furlong*, Tom Roberts; and *Hillside*, Arthur Streeton.

This gallery is found in the 1905-built Police Courts where one court room and two adjoining cells have been preserved. Several works by English artist Stanley Spencer are also here, as well as the one painting that's probably known to every WA schoolchild,

Right: stained-glass window, Art Gallery of WA

for content if not quality. *The Foundation of Perth* by George Morrison Pitt catches that magic moment when Mrs Dance marked the founding of Perth by attacking a tree with an axe. More recent Australian art, up to 1960, is displayed in the upper area.

In the main building's first floor are two galleries of aboriginal art, bark paintings and carvings, and Imaginings, the contemporary art collection. There are some powerful works here. Don't miss *Allegory: after Courbet* by John de Andrea. Allow a while, because you'll want to stare and wait for them to move, convinced the life-size figure of Andrea and his model are real. Aboriginal art has its own power, and mystery. It takes a while to appreciate subtle differences in style. Watch for works by Jimmy Pike, Paddy Tjamitji, Rover Thomas and Butcher Cherel Janangoo.

The Art Gallery Café is good for a light lunch, sitting with a big wine glass watching the parade thronging to and from the station. But with limited time, another option is a quick dip into Northbridge. The culture concourse is a mall extension of James Street, and only William Street separates culture and Perth's racy sector.

The Brass Monkey (corner William/James streets) is a definitive new-look Australian pub in a beautiful Victorian building. The best bar is upstairs, with excellent wine and beers; the balcony overlooking the bustling lunchtime street is *the* place to drink. You could lunch well here, but move on down James Street if you like Asian food. Shop names are the clue to the ethnic waves that have swept through **Northbridge** *(see page 58)* since the war. The older ones were Italian and Greek, while more recent are the migrants from Vietnam, Malaysia, Singapore and China. **Old Shanghai** is 200m (219yds) from The Brass Monkey, a food hall that's clean and civilised; prices are ridiculously low, and there's even a bar.

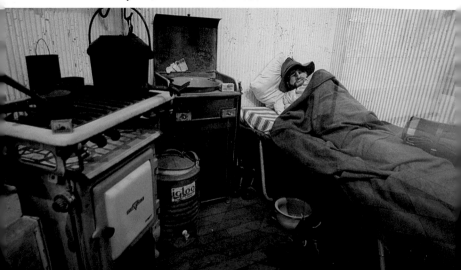

Shop Stops

If the Northbridge side of the tracks is for entertainment, the south side's for shopping. So cross over at the Horseshoe Bridge on William Street and return to Forrest Chase, where the buskers should be in full swing. Ragtime pianist John Gill is one to watch for among a throng of jugglers, mimes, living statues and other performers. Between the Chase and St Georges Terrace, a warren of malls and arcades has all the regular shops, and many specialising in good value, genuine Australian stuff. In Carillon Arcade, look for **Showbits** (tel: 08-9321 2596) for off-beat paraphernalia; and **R M Williams** (tel: 08-9321 7786) 'bushman's outfitter' for stylish and substantial kits, from boots, saddles and whips to hats and swags (bed-rolls).

There are food halls in many of the arcades, including below ground at Carillon. Up higher, on the second floor, is **Sassellas Tavern** (tel: 08-9322 4001), a bar and bistro which might be welcome later. Sushi shops are popular in Perth. One of the best is **Jaws Kaiten Sushi** (tel: 08-9481 1445) in Hay Street Mall, where you sit at a counter and are served by a continuous conveyor belt, and pay according to the colour of the serving dish selected.

London Court must be seen. A 1930s-built Tudor replica, it's better than it sounds. The authentic feel is enhanced by the narrow alley, with bijou shops and decorative porticos at each end, one in Hay Street Mall and the other on St Georges Terrace. It's the right place for antiques and jewellery: fancy hats and stuff at **Passchendale's Accessories** (tel: 08-9325 8309); high-quality wool and cotton clothes at **Purely Australian** and the amazing coloured Argyle Diamonds at **Swan Diamonds** (tel: 08-9325 8166). Argyle diamonds are unique to WA, mined 3,000km (1,864 miles) north at Lake Argyle. Some stones are white, ranging to yellow, champagne and the rare pink.

Other Purely Australian shops, like the bigger one in Murray Street Mall, stock a wider range of Aussie icons, such as the Driza-Bone waxed stockman's coat and the fur-felt Akubra hat. You'll also see these at **Outback Red** (tel: 08-9325 5151; Plaza Arcade, between Hay and Murray malls) plus the Thomas Cook range. They also have lightweight hats, leather coats, bags, and a women's version of the Driza-Bone (in pink!).

For the average Aussie bloke, this kind of marathon day – 'exhibition legs' syndrome combined with shopping – builds a mighty thirst. Well, sink a drink and carry on sightseeing or better yet, sit and watch Perth whirl by while dining in style at the top of St Martin's Tower, 44 St Georges Terrace, in the **C Restaurant Lounge** revolving restaurant (tel: 08-9220 8333). It's open every day for dinner from 6pm, and lunch Sunday to Friday. By arriving at 6pm you can see all of Perth, from ocean to hills, in daylight and then see the City of Light switch on. A complete revolution takes 85 minutes. The cocktail bar is a good place to start, while the grand piano soothes your over-stretched plastic cards.

Top left: 'Don't worry, be happy' – busker in Murray Street Mall
Left: the 'bushman's outfitter', R M Williams. **Above:** Murray Street Mall

4. FREMANTLE *(see map, p47)*

Although this itinerary suggests highlights that can be covered in a morning, Fremantle (Freo) is worth a whole holiday by itself. A vibrant port city, Freo has history and heritage, art and culture – and is a lot of fun.

A ferry from Perth to Freo takes an hour or so. Captain Cook Cruises (tel: 08-9325 3341) costs around A$11 one-way, including commentary, tea/coffee; or if returning Freo/Perth, wine tasting. A tram runs from the jetty to the city centre, and various tram tours of the whole city are available. If your schedule is tight, go there on the train, alight at Fremantle station and follow this circuit, to cover some sights in half-day.

If you decide to hoof it, start your Fremantle circuit at the Round House and Tunnel (anyone will point you in the right direction). The **Round House** (daily 10am–3.30pm) is WA's oldest public building and first gaol, built in 1830 at Arthur Head, which is where Captain Fremantle planted the Union Jack and claimed Western Australia. The Whalers' Tunnel was cut through in 1837. Government funds have been promised to renovate the Round House and reopen the tunnel.

Walking towards the ocean from the city centre, you'll soon be aware of the hundreds of heritage buildings lining the streets. Fremantle is the world's best preserved example of a 19th-century port streetscape, according to the experts who know. Defence of The America's Cup in yacht racing off Fremantle in 1987 brought world attention to the port. The renovation started then, and has never stopped. Bustling with alfresco cafés, museums, galleries, pubs, markets and shops, Fremantle is at its liveliest on weekends.

Top: Fremantle streetscape – straight out of a 19th-century novel
Left: roaring forth

Colonial Architecture

As you re-cross the railway after the Round House, look out for early 19th century architecture in Phillimore Street – the old Fire Station at No 18, the Chamber of Commerce at No 16, and the Old Customs House at the corner of Cliff Street. Follow Cliff Street for another, the Samson Building at No 31. At No 4 Cliff Street is the former maritime museum, now known as the **Shipwreck Galleries** (tel: 08-9431 8444; www.mm.wa.gov.au; daily 9.30am–5pm), its huge collection including shipwreck relics dating back to the 17th century. (Note: at time of press, the new WA Maritime Museum opened at Victoria Quay, a short walk away. Details found at the same website above.) Turn into Mouat Street at the end of Croke Lane for the Georgian Old Court House at the corner of Marine Terrace, which operated from 1884 until 1897, and the 1903 Water Police Barracks at No 10 Marine Terrace.

Walking along Marine Terrace, look across the Esplanade lawns to the **Fishing Boat Harbour**, anchorage for a 500-strong fleet. Lots of smaller restaurants, and bigger ones operated by the fishing companies, are right here. Return for lunch later; now cross the railway just past Suffolk Street. Sit on the jetty outside **Cicerello's** or one of the others restaurants, and enjoy fresh Freo fish. For an even classier (and more expensive) meal, **Sails** (tel: 08-9430 5050) is recommended, with an ocean viewing upstairs deck.

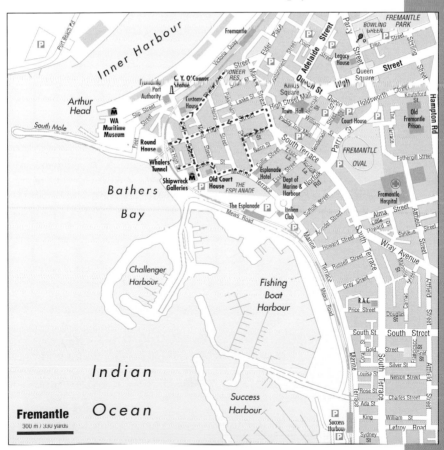

city itineraries

Cappuccino Strip

After the Water Police Barracks, you could look in for Broome pearls at
Artisans of the Sea (tel: 08-9336 3633), at the corner of Marine Terrace
and Collie Street. Pearls and jewellery from Broome, in the state's far north,
are now part of a legitimate industry, but in 1861 Aborigines were forced to
dive for pearl shell by white traders.
By 1886, when the Aborigines Protection Act was passed, up to 700
were working on the pearl luggers.
As well as pearls for sale, Artisans
of the Sea has heritage displays and
a video on modern pearling.

Dominating the ocean front is the
Esplanade Hotel (08-9432 4000).
Modern extensions blend into the original facade, built in gold-rush 1890s
style like many Fremantle hotels. Head inland past the hotel along Essex
Street to reach Freo's famed 'Cappuccino Strip' on South Terrace. Alfresco
is *de rigeur* here, it seems. No other place in WA makes as much of the
Mediterranean climate. All along the Strip, people eat, drink or dawdle over
coffee for hours on end and watch the street entertainers. You'd think they
were on the Mediterranean, and good on 'em! Italian influence says you'll
find the best coffee in the state here.

There's also some of the best beer, across Marine Terrace at the **Sail and
Anchor** (tel: 08-9335 8433), one of the boutique pub breweries serving
brews such as Redback and the fiercely strong Dogbolter. Alongside the
pub are the **Fremantle Markets** (tel: 08-9335 3120; Mon–Fri 9am–9pm; Sat
9am–5pm; Sun 10am–5pm), first set up in 1897 and National Trust-listed.
Handmade bric-a-brac, antiques, fashion, food and spices mingle in a glorious mélange within the gold rush building. Don't miss the market, but do
save some money for a bunch of worthy arties further down the Strip, and
maybe the buskers who entertain there. They usually pull a crowd in the wide
mall between pub and markets. A few coins are always welcome.

Crafts Browsing

Fremantle is a creative haven, so walk back past the pub to Bannister and High streets. **Staircase Gallery** (tel: 08-9430 6447) has sculpture and carvings of native timbers by leading artisans; **Bannister Street Craftworks** (tel: 08-9336 2035) is a showplace for many more. **Desert Designs Japingka Gallery** (tel: 08-9430 4332) specialises in paintings and limited edition prints by Aboriginal artists. More can be seen further along at No 43 High Street in **Bellamy's Oceanic Art Gallery** (tel: 08-9430 7439), and at **Creative Native**, No 63 High Street.

If you can spend more time in Fremantle, there's plenty to do. The **E Shed Markets** on Victoria Quay have more than 60 speciality shops, an international food court and live entertainment. Victoria Quay, near where you started at the Round House, also has the **New Maritime Museum** (daily 9.30am–5pm) at Arthur Head and the wonderful Sail Training Ship *Leeuwin*, the 55-m (180-ft) three-masted barquentine. You might even book a half-day sail.

Nightlife is extensive too, with lots of music of all kinds in the pubs, and clubs like the **Fly By Night Musicians' Club** at Queen Street (tel: 08-9430 5976) hosting international jazz and blues. Music venues and entertainers are all listed in the Friday edition of *West Australian*. **Fremantle Tourist Bureau** at King's Square, High Street, (tel: 08-9431 7878) will have all the information you need.

5. WINERIES OF SWAN VALLEY *(see map, p51)*

Sample some of Western Australia's best wine labels during your morning tour of Swan Valley, the birthplace of West Australian wine, and now among the world's best; also take in the Caversham Wildlife Park, fine crafts shops and restaurants. Some wineries close on Mon and Tue.

There are two ways to go – by car or boat. Driving through the wine country with the wind in your hair could add a lot of enjoyment to the trip. Executive Hire Cars (tel: 08-9421 1550; www.executive.com.au) has self-drive sports and other cars for daily hire. The police are tough on drink-driving and random breath testing is widespread. If you plan a lot of tastings, either appoint a light-drinking skipper, or rent a car and driver. Ash Craft (tel: 0407 993 215) hires himself and his London black cab at around A$65 an hour. Negotiate for longer trips. Or try the regular taxi firms like Swan, and Black and White. By river, Captain Cook Cruises (tel: 08-9325 3341; www.captaincookcruises.com.au) offers a half-day trip to Olive Farm (1.45–5.30pm); or full day (9.45am–4.45pm) to Houghton and Sandalford, with lunch at Bells Estate.

WA's historical beginnings as wine country dates back to 1829, when Botanist Thomas Walters planted the first vines at Olive Farm; WA's first wine was produced 5 years later. Such early interest in the finer things of life says much for WA. Even Captain Fremantle had the grape in mind when he claimed the state. His diary records planting South African cuttings in the garden at Arthur Head, when preparing camp for the settlers. But it took 150 years for wine to become a modern WA success story.

Guildford, around 12km (7.5 miles) from Perth, is at the start of the Swan Valley and worth a stop during your tour. It is an early settler town with many antique shops and period pubs. Cross the railway at the Post Office tower to follow West Swan Road on a loop through the valley. A heritage area just over the lines includes the Courthouse and Old Gaol in **Guildford Museum** (tel: 08-9279 1891), which will open by appointment, and **St Matthew's Church**, with an original moat still on three sides. It was built in 1873, replacing the original destroyed by fire a year earlier during a christening.

Nearby is **Rose and Crown Hotel** (tel: 08-9279 8444), where the **Inchant Brewing Company** (www.bullantbeer.com) range includes bitter, light, porter and even ginger beer. There's also Dutch Bock Bier, spicy Fettled Beer and several other very distinctive brews. Some are available on draught at the hotel but don't over indulge as there is one more winery to go.

Sandalford Winery

As you drive along West Swan Road past Lilac Hill, with the Midland Guildford cricket ground on the right, you're into the vines. There are many wineries to visit – go into any one that appeals – but **Sandalford** (tel: 08-9374 9374; www.sandalford.com; daily 10am–5pm) is a solid start. It's one of WA's best established, set up in 1840. All the wineries have tastings and cellar-door sales, but big ones like Sandalford also offer wine-making and 'exclusive tasting' tours. They also make a wider range than some small vineyards, and have wines from their vineyards in other WA regions.

For a break between sips, after Sandalford turn off the main road to **Caversham Wildlife Park** (tel: 08-9274 2202; www.cavershamwildlife.com.au; daily 9am–5pm) at the corner of Arthur and Cranleigh streets, and its menagerie of native animals, wild and woolly or furry and cuddly.

Back on West Swan Road, over the next few kilometres the choices are wide and varied. There's local produce, honey and fruit for sale, as well as

Aboriginal art displays, tea rooms, vineyards, tourist villages, golf ranges and more. Drive slowly and take your pick, but don't eat too much because the biggest treat of the day could be waiting if you lunch at Lamont.

You might compare the new **Duckstein Brewery**, No 9720 West Swan Road (tel: 08-9296 0620; Wed–Sun 11am–10pm), with the range of beers at the earlier Inchant brewery. Both are fairly new to the valley, riding on a frothy wave of crafted beer success that has rolled out the barrel in other popular wine areas of WA. Duckstein makes German-style beer and also has a restaurant. All beer is served direct from the maturing tank.

Lamont Winery

When the road makes a t-junction with Great Northern Highway, approximately 9km (6 miles) from Caversham Wildlife Park, turn right, watch for a left turn at Haddrill Road, and follow the signs for **Lamont Winery** (tel: 08-9296 4485; www.lamonts.com.au; Wed–Sun 10am–5pm), turning right at Moore Road and again into Bisdee Road.

The Lamont family involvement with wine and the valley goes back three generations. They began making wine on their own property in the 1970s, cellar door sales started in 1978, and the restaurant opened in 1989. King Street Food and Wine, on St Georges Terrace, sells Lamont produce and the newest venture is a restaurant overlooking the Swan, in east Perth. Kate Lamont's food column in *The Australian* has spread the family's fame far and wide.

Sit out and gaze across the vines with a glass of chardonnay or cabernet in hand. The alfresco food costs A$10–15 per plate. Lunch in the restaurant (you should book) costs around A$45 per head for three courses.

Depart Lamont and head down the highway for **Talijancich** at Hyem Road (tel: 08-9296 4289; www.taliwine. com.au; Mon–Fri 9am–5pm). Now producing superb verdelho, semillon, riesling and shiraz, the family began production 65 years ago and built a successful business on fortified wines like muscat and liqueur hermitage.

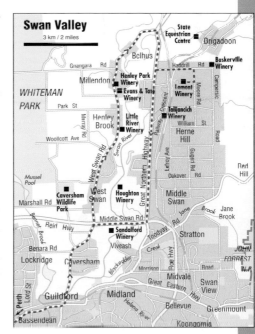

Left: good to the last drop
Above: Swan Valley grape vine

Yet Another Winery

Houghton Wines, Dale Road (tel: 08-9274 9540; www.brlhardy.com.au; daily 10am–5pm), could be your next stop, right, off the highway. Another big company with grounds so extensive they draw thousands to an annual jazz festival, Houghton produces the best selling bottled wine in Australia – the white burgundy, created in 1937 by the legendary Jack Mann, grandfather of the Lamont dynasty. Inexpensive, it matures in the bottle and is bought to keep by many buffs. Some is kept back and matured as a blue-labelled show reserve. Both are good buys. After Houghton, a right turn at Middle Swan Road will connect again with West Swan Road for a return to Guildford, where those antique and bric-a-brac shops await.

Other worthy vineyards on this route include Little River (tel: 08-9296 4462), Swanbrook (tel: 08-9296 3100), Henley Park (08-9296 4328), Mann Winery (tel: 08-9296 4348) and Baskerville (tel: 08-9296 1348). **Swan Valley Tourist Information Centre** (tel: 08-9250 4400) has details and maps.

6. WHALE WATCHING AND THE AQUARIUM OF WESTERN AUSTRALIA (AQWA) *(see map, p52)*

Take a morning to watch giant humpback whales swimming offshore. These monsters migrate to colder Antarctic waters in spring and can be seen all along the western coast from Exmouth to Albany. While at Sorrento Quay area, visit the AQWA for more marine choices.

If you have a car, take the freeway north, exit at Hepburn Avenue and follow signs for Hillarys Boat Harbour and Sorrento Quay. The cost of a taxi is around A$30. Or else buy a Transperth combined train/bus ticket at the central station in Wellington Street and travel north to Stirling or Warwick stations. From there, the 423 bus runs right into Hillarys Boat Harbour.

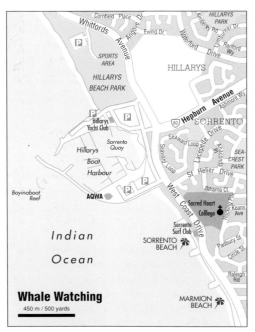

Whale Watching
450 m / 500 yards

The best way to see giant humpback whales is up close from a boat navigated by an experienced skipper. **AQWA** (www.aqwa. com.au; tel: 08-9447 7500; daily 10am–5pm; Dec–April 10am–9pm; Oct and Nov on Wed, Sat and Sun only) has expanded its service, offering an eye-to-eye experience with the whales from small boats. Another option is a 2-hour cruise with **Hillarys Fast Ferries**. This

company uses bigger craft, but will collect you from Perth, or Scarborough (wwwhillarysfastferrics.com.au, tel: 08-9246 1039. Whether you enjoy being on, in or around the ocean, Sorrento Quay offers many marine choices.

At AQWA, you can choose to go underwater without getting wet, enclosed in a 98-m (322-ft) long acrylic tunnel. As you travel slowly on a moving walkway, sharks, seals, rays and hundreds of other fish swim over and around you in a massive natural environment tank.

Of course, if you would like to swim with the sharks, you can do so when they're fed (feedings are twice a day). All you need is a scuba-diving certificate and lots of nerve! More soothing is the touching pool; more exciting the outdoor dolphin pool, where these intriguing mammals put on a feeding-time show thrice daily. Poisonous and exotic fish, saltwater crocodiles, marine souvenirs and all the other tourist paraphernalia are on display, too. Call AQWA for timing details and to check entry prices.

Fishing Trips

Fishing charters can be taken from the harbour but you need to book in advance. **Mills Fishing Charters** (tel: 08-9246 5334) charge A$75 per weekday per person, A$85 at weekends, and supply all equipment and bait. You keep all you catch, gutted and cleaned for you. An early start is needed – charter is from 6.30am to approximately 4pm.

Another option is a twilight cruise with Hillarys Fast Ferries *(details above)*, up and down the coast (6–8pm) right through summer, or a longer trip to Rottnest, stepping ashore for refreshments (2.30–6.30pm).

Ferries to Rottnest Island run daily, and real boaties will enjoy the hundreds of boats moored and on sale. Landlubbers will also enjoy Sorrento Quay, which features restaurants, a pub, shops and a small funfair during school holidays. **Jetty's** smorgasbord is excellent value for a big lunch; so is the **Café Brasserie**, with wide-ranging food choices and a hamburger bar. Children will enjoy the shallow water beach, water slide and funfair.

Above: close-up encounters with fascinating sharks at AQWA

7. KINGS PARK *(see map, p18–19)*

Perth's pride and joy, this hilltop park of bushland and botanic gardens is ideal for a morning or afternoon meander. Choose the afternoon if you intend to stay for the drama in the park at dusk; performances usually held in December and January.

Travel by bus or train to Wellington Street, walk through William Street to St Georges Terrace and take any bus (free) west along the Terrace to the Fraser Avenue entrance to the park.

WA is famous for its magnificent wildflowers, which are a major tourist attraction. The richest areas are sandplains or heaths, which botanists know by the Aboriginal name *Kwongan*. One of the best is north of Perth, which has a range of small trees, shrubs and flowers. Feather flowers, leschenaultia, dryandra, grevillea, wattle (mimosa) and myrtles are but a few of the genus.

If you have no time for a tour of the country, **Kings Park** is a 400-hectare (988-acre) microcosm of the Australian bush. In spring, the park comes alive in a riot of colours and scents, and puts on quite a show for visitors. Orchids, kangaroo paws, banksias and countless more grow right through the park. For the rest of the year the park stays green, but winter rain encourages more growth and makes the sand trails firmer and easier to walk. In the 17-hectare (42-acre) **Botanic Gardens**, varieties from eastern Australia and other Mediterranean climes share space with West Australian species.

Bush Trails

Most visitors, even locals, don't know or use the sand and limestone bush trails that criss-cross the park. They keep to the playgrounds, picnic areas, the botanic gardens and the rest. Large as these are, they cover a relatively small area, leaving the trails quiet with a secluded, almost private atmosphere. The vegetation is dense, threaded with colour in spring but always fascinating. More than 70 bird species have been recorded in Kings Park, colourful parrots included. It supports small mammals, insects and reptiles, including snakes, though rarely seen. Keep to the trails and be watchful, especially in spring.

Pick up a free map from the **Visitor Information Centre** (tel: 08-9480 3634; www.bgpa.wa.gov.au) at the Fraser Avenue entrance and you will appreciate the scope of the park, which was first established in 1872, with 175 hectares (432 acres). It seems amazing that a site so close to the city

Above: free entertainment at Kings Park. **Top right:** colourful wildflowers
Right: jacaranda in full bloom

survived development, but it grew, being gazetted at the present size in 1895. The only threat to Kings Park now is bush fire, and you'll probably see evidence of the most recent one. Fortunately the Bush has developed immunity, many species flourishing in the aftermath of a blaze as their long-dormant seeds open in the heat.

It's enjoyable to wander around, but you'll get more from a short visit by joining the free guided walks conducted by volunteers every day from April to October, and weekly from November to March. These experts will either take you through the Botanic Gardens or on a nature walk. The Visitor Information Centre has full data on the options. All start at the Karri log in Fraser Avenue, where nearby are the display glass houses and the Rare and Endangered Garden. Beautiful resource though it is, Kings Park is more than just a tourist attraction. Scientists here are involved in research, conservation and propagation. They comb the state for rare and unusual species and use the park in part as a nursery.

The greenhouses provide a fascinating insight into the work done by the scientists. Also close to Fraser Avenue are the new water gardens, often used as a venue for the annual Shakespeare in the Park production. Generally a fun production – *Midsummer Night's Dream*, *Romeo and Juliet* have been past shows – this starts at dusk, usually in December and January. Check dates and times with the park, but booking isn't necessary most nights. Bring a picnic, lounge on a rug and round out the day. Art lovers can also catch an Aboriginal artist at work in the Artists in Residence gallery.

8. COTTESLOE BEACH *(see map, p56)*

Spend a morning exploring one of Western Australia's most popular and fashionable 'resort' beaches, built around the seaside town of Cottesloe.

Take the train from Wellington Street; alight at Cottesloe station.

Cottesloe is a solid and well-established small town of only 7,000 residents and superior dwellings in a short coastal strip. The towering Norfolk pines you'll see on most streets have become something of an icon, a long-lasting symbol of the town. Many houses are in the turn-of-the-19th century 'Federation' style, tastefully mixed in with modern developments.

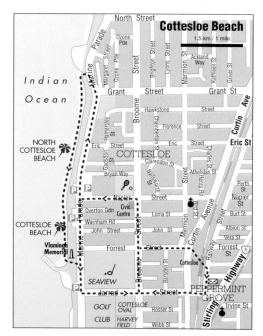

At Cottesloe station, cross the railway line on Jarrad Street and walk west towards the ocean. Jarrad Street will take you right through the Seaview Golf Course to the ocean, but stop short of the links and turn right on Broome Street to see the most splendid council offices in the state.

Civic Centre

The **Civic Centre** shouldn't work, but somehow it does. Walk through the gates, wander around the grounds and observe. This is a 1911 Spanish-style mansion within Gothic balustraded garden walls, and set in spacious ter-

Above: the national pastime – surfing

raced gardens. Tycoon Claude de Bernales built the villa, wrapping it around the 1898 home of a one-time WA attorney-general. The grounds and walls date back to the original. As the buildings are in daily use by council staff they aren't open to the public, but if you ask nicely someone might show you through the fantastic timbered interior that's become Council Chambers.

Nobody will object if you wish to linger in the elevated gardens, a wonderful place to stop and enjoy views of the Indian Ocean, distant Rottnest Island, and the busy shipping lane into Fremantle.

Napier Street, alongside the north wall, will take you down to the ocean and Marine Parade. Turn to walk along the front, past pubs, cafés, restaurants and shops towards **Indiana Tea Rooms** (tel: 08-9385 5005), a beautiful pavilion right on the beach *(see below)*. This is the most popular part of Cottesloe Beach, with a paddling pool, volleyball courts and good swimming. Cottesloe has more in common with European-style seaside resorts than most WA beaches. Tourist facilities, plenty of parking, toilets and change rooms and the rest draw visitors from all over the metropolis. The beach is also popular with early-morning keep-fit oldies, body surfers, swimmers and particularly, families. You can avoid the crowds by using other parts of the beach – there's plenty of sand to spare. The town buys more each year – top-grade only! – to replace that washed away by winter storms.

But remember that swimming in Australia can be rugged. There will probably be lifeguards on duty, so swim where they can see you, between the red flags on the beach. If you're unsure about conditions, ask lifeguards for advice, or talk to the Council rangers whose office is below the tea rooms.

Cottesloe is one of Perth's finest older suburbs. The people are anxious to preserve the town's style, so despite the British heritage you'll find none of the tacky seaside excesses of the northern hemisphere. Two cafés, **Blue Duck** (tel: 08-9385 2499) and **Barchetta**, are beachside of Marine Parade, giving great views and good food. Several more, such as **Beaches** (tel: 08-9384 4412), are of similar high standard, with sidewalk tables on the other side of the Parade. Of the two pubs **Cottesloe Beach Hotel** is the most attractive, a place where you can sit and enjoy a drink with ocean glimpses.

For an elegant lunch, Indiana Tea Rooms is hard to pass up. It's probably wise to book; try for a table by the big front windows which rack up wide to admit the skies. Spicy Asian cuisine predominates, but you can just have coffee and snacks, too.

When returning to the station, you could live dangerously and walk through the golf course along Jarrad Street. Look out for flying balls, you can keep all you catch.

Right: charming Cottesloe Beach Hotel has nice ocean views

9. NORTHBRIDGE *(see map, p33)*

Reserve Northbridge – the most mediterranean part of Perth – for strolling in the early evening, sidewalk dining and dawdling as you watch the passing parade.

If you're staying in central Perth, just walk across the Horseshoe Bridge and you're in the heart of Northbridge. Buses and trains to Wellington Street will deposit you at the bridge.

A good place to start is where Lake and James streets meet, at the hub of the district where 'petrol-heads' with their motorbikes congregate. Tables and chairs cover three of the corners. Sit on the sidewalk with some wine or coffee and take Northbridge's pulse. North along Lake Street, the **Elephant and Wheelbarrow** pub is another place to sit out. Security staff will check if you're old enough to drink, then you can sample the mock-Tudor comforts, and newer ales and stouts.

Wining and Dining

Other good pubs are the **Brass Monkey** at eastern end of James Street; **The Deen** in Aberdeen Street which has several spaces with live bands, nightclub and chill out areas; and **Rosie O'Grady's** at the western end. The Irish-inspired Rosie's is opposite Russell Square, a traditional meeting place for Aborigines, but today gentrified with nearby town houses and the St James apartment hotel. Upgrading the square also rejuvenated the central bandstand. Take a look at the carved fountains all around it, with Aussie bush icons cast in bronze.

On the corner of Francis Street, on the east side, the dome of the **Greek Orthodox Cathedral** marks another aspect of Australia's multi-culture that's

so apparent in Northbridge. The best established community, after the Aborigines and the Anglo-Saxons, are the mediterranean Europeans who began influencing Oz culture as migrants after World War II. The next important wave was Asian, and the little Chinatown at the east end of James and Roe streets displays their influence. Alfresco eating at **Old Shanghai** on James Street is excellent and very affordable.

Before dinner, visit the **Grapeskin** wine bar, part of the Brass Monkey *(see above)* but with a separate entrance on William Street. Fine and expensive wines are sold by the large glassful here, and with

Above: pub sign. **Left:** The Brass Monkey. **Right:** the good life

some costing up to A\$60 a bottle it's a great way to sample a wide range.

Grapeskin is an excellent example of the kind of upmarket wine bars now flourishing in Perth. It was a long time coming. Not so long ago, 'wine bar' was a suspect phrase harking back to the days of winos and red noses.

While restaurants of all kinds flourish in Northbridge, Italian-style eateries predominate. **Mamma Maria's** (tel: 08-9328 4532) was one of the earliest. Along James Street you can sit outside many, such as **Vino Vino** (tel: 08-9328 5403). Nearby **Paradiso Cinema** is a small independent moviehouse with multi-screens, and has found a niche that accommodates both arthouse and quality mainstream movies.

Northbridge is a delight to stroll in, look at and enjoy. Normal street manners and awareness should be enough to keep you safe, but as the night progresses take more care. Police patrols, on foot and in vehicles, are more obvious in Northbridge than any other part of town. Along William Street are many more cafés, but the more risque establishments are further north. Plain walls, but no red lights, conceal shady Northbridge by night.

Varied Entertainment

Clubs along Lake Street keep on metamorphosing. No matter the name, the young people queue for entry. Just past the Elephant and Wheelbarrow is the Church, which has had at least four name changes in the past decade.

All the dance clubs cater mainly for younger customers but one of the best for a broader audience is **Metro City** on Roe Street (tel: 08-9228 0500). The state-of-the-art building is a concert club with many viewing levels. Big acts frequently make an appearance here, so it's worth checking the programme first.

Plans to sink the railway that divides Northbridge from the CBD mean that Wellington and Murray streets could eventually become 'Northbridge South'! For nightclub fun, it's worth crossing the tracks to Murray Street anyway. There, the **Spirit Sound Bar** is one of the most avant-garde, and the **Factory Dance Club**, **Amplifier Bar** and **Belgian Beer Café** all compete.

Excursions

EXCURSION 1. ROTTNEST ISLAND *(see map, p62)*

Make an early start for this all-day trip to Perth's popular wildlife reserve, just off the coast.

Getting there is part of the fun. Fast ferries leave daily from Fremantle, Hillarys Boat Harbour or the Barrack Street Jetty in Perth. First ferry departs Fremantle at 7am, and the last leaves Rottnest at 5.30pm, except on Friday when there is a 8pm boat. A fast ferry will have you there in an hour, and all operators offer day trips of various kinds. Operators are: Rottnest Express (tel: 08-9335 6406; www.rottnestexpress.com.au); Rottnest Ferry Oceanic Cruises (tel: 08-9325 1191; www.oceaniccruises.com.au) and Hillary's Fast Ferries (08-9246 1039; www.hillarysfastferries.com.au). Once a year some hundreds of people leap into water at Freo and swim across. Others take the ferry, then run round the island four times to make up the marathon distance. If either of these methods appeal call the Dept of Sport and Recreation (tel: 08 9387 9700, www.dsr.gov.au) for details.

Rottnest is only 18km (11 miles) off the coast. On a clear day, you can see it from the Perth beaches. At night, the lighthouse flashes bright across to Perth. A day is never enough, according to the old Rotto hands. But with an early start you can make the most of it, sightsee all round the island by bus or bike, feed the 'quokkas' and yourself, swim, snorkel and enjoy the sunshine. With luck you'll take a little time, stroll around the quiet roads, ease up and relax on the beach. Then maybe you'll have an inkling of why Rottnest has been a favourite holiday place for generations of 'Westralians'.

The island is a great leveller. Many of the regulars who book their 2 weeks every year leave air-conditioned luxury homes in Perth to 'rough it on Rotto'. It takes a while to wind down, but then you wouldn't know if your neighbour in the chalet next door is a millionaire or just like the rest of us.

Balancing the preservation of Rottnest with the needs of tourism isn't easy. In the busy summer season there's never enough accommodation at the single hotel, chalets or even in tents. Many people sail across, but moorings are limited, too.

The **Rottnest Visitor and Information Centre** (tel: 08-9372 9752; www. rottnest.wa.gov.au) should be your first port of call, for up to-date information about travel to the island, bus and train trips, hire facilities and things to do (book ahead for the 2-hour island tour).

Left: Rottnest Island view from Oliver Hill
Right: an Australian quokka

Only 200–300 people live on Rottnest, and the school has just 25 pupils. Private cars aren't allowed, but there are service vehicles and a bus which will take you around Rottnest in about an hour. But the universal transport is the hire bike, which you can fix up once you land. Snorkel and scuba gear can be hired from **Malibu Dive** (tel: 08-9292 5111; www.rottnest diving.com.au).

Main Attractions

Swimming and snorkelling off Rottnest is a must-do. Warmed by the Leeuwin current flowing from the far north, the clear water is always a few degrees warmer than off the mainland. Rocky formations and coral are fascinating to swim around, with shoals of colourful fish, and there are places where you can dive through rock arches and tunnels.

Another must is to meet the quokkas, rare small creatures found almost everywhere on Rottnest, which owes its very name to these brown furry wallabies. It's a pity that Dutch explorers, the first to find and name the island, mistook them for rodents.

Rottnest has a past, of course, including dark times, with an Aboriginal prison and a wartime military base. A narrow-gauge railway takes visitors

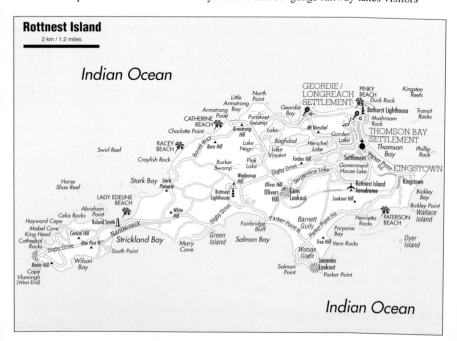

up Oliver Hill to the old military fort, where tunnels and guns are still in place.

Island food and drink are all found at Thomson Bay, where the ferries berth. The only pub is the **Rottnest Hotel** (known as 'The Quokka Arms') and includes Vlamingh's Restaurant. Another restaurant is at **The Lodge** nearby; simple meals are served at **Rottnest Tea Rooms** and **Dome**.

EXCURSION 2. NEW NORCIA AND THE PINNACLES
(see map, p64)

This northern trip provides a taste of Australian countryside as you travel to the historic monastery town of New Norcia or the spectacular limestone Pinnacles. Either excursion can be handled in a day, but to cover both you need to plan for an overnighter.

From Perth, head for Guildford and Midland to pick up Northern Highway. At Muchea, you choose: stay with Northern Highway if you're heading for New Norcia or fork left on Brand Highway for the Pinnacles. Follow Brand Highway and look for signs for Cervantes, which is 245km (152 miles) north of Perth. If you don't want to drive, book a lightning one-day New Norcia/Pinnacles coach tour or an exciting 4-wheel drive of the Pinnacles, including a ride on the sand dunes. Check with the WA Visitor Centre (tel: 1300 361 351; www.westernaustralia.net) for details.

New Norcia

Driving in WA is relatively stress-free, traffic is light and roads are good. Hazards are few, but keep a watch for kangaroos – and road-trains. These are long-distance trucks with two or three trailers in tow. Bright yellow signs warn of kangaroos in the vicinity, and their corpses by the highway are a graphic reminder. Kangaroos are active as the day cools down and they sometimes wander onto the road, so drive carefully when it's getting dark.

Northern Highway leads directly to New Norcia, a Benedictine mission founded by monks led by Spaniards Dom Rosendo Salvado and Dom Jose Serra in 1846. Salvado was the man whose superlative piano skills raised funds and united the Perth community to support the mission. Serra was also to become the second Catholic archbishop of Perth.

The New Norcia mission brought a piece of old Spain to the pastoral area, inhabited then only by indigenous Aborigines. Its architecture is remarkable by any standard, the small town a triumph of civilising influences. It is only 132km (82 miles) from Perth, and you will have plenty of time to enjoy the countryside, lunch in New Norcia and follow its Heritage Trail. This easy 2-km (1-miles) walk includes the monastery, museum, art gallery and more. At the museum and gallery, a monk conducts a free tour on most afternoons, showing the collection of 16th- and 17th-century old masters and Australian artists.

Left: Rottnest's warm waters beckon
Right: New Norcia mission

For many years monks ran the Catholic College. The school is now closed – another victim of the dwindling country population in Australia – but the Gothic and Byzantine buildings remain to be admired. The New Norcia Monastery is not open to the general public, but visitors are welcome to look in at the gate and make enquiries at the office.

Other historic points of interest on the trail are the Abbey church, cemetery, the Beehouse, the old flour mill, Bishop Salvado's statue, Bishop's Well and more. A 'new' flour mill was built in 1879 and remains one of the oldest operating in the state. New Norcia bakery products are sold at a premium price in Perth. Lunch or dinner can be had either at **New Norcia Hotel** (tel: 08-9654 8034), or the **New Norcia Roadhouse** (tel: 08-9654 8020; 7.30am–8.30pm).

The elegant buildings and surroundings of the monastery are in marked contrast to the natural environment of the Pinnacles. Seeing both in a day isn't feasible, but you might consider staying at the New Norcia Hotel and driving on to Cervantes next day.

Pinnacles

Thousands of limestone pillars rising from a stark landscape of yellow sands near **Cervantes** are one of the state's most fascinating natural wonders. Dutch sailors see-

Above: the stunning Pinnacles

ing the 5-m (16-ft) high pillars from the ocean thought they were the remains of an ancient civilisation. Slanting light in the early morning or late afternoon shows them best, creating eerie shadows and a desolate moonscape effect.

The **Pinnacles** are in Nambung National Park, 6km (3¾ mile) inland and 17km (10½ miles) south from Cervantes, a small town excised from the park to serve people in the local crayfishing industry. A small charge is made to enter the Pinnacles, where you drive on a one-way loop through the dune desert. Another walk loop starts at the car park. Fishing is popular at nearby Hangover Bay or Kangaroo Point. Food and drink should be available in Cervantes, but it's a long drive from Perth, so carry drinks with you.

EXCURSION 3. MARGARET RIVER *(see map, p66)*

Ideally, set aside 2 days to explore the wineries and the magnificent surf breaks, coastal cliffs and limestone caves of the Margaret River region.

Hire a car for this excursion. From Perth, follow the freeway south to its end and turn right on Thomas Road, to a t-junction with Highway 1, where you turn left. Stay alert for another left turn a few kilometres on, which skirts Rockingham and takes you via Mandurah to Bunbury. At Bunbury, stay on 1, now called South Western Highway, for the scenic route. This will go inland to Boyanup, Donnybrook and Dalingup. This scenic section makes Perth/Margaret River 350km (218 miles) – about 4 to 5 hours' driving. The more direct route to Margaret River follows the coast on the Bussel Highway. Signs should show Busselton and Margaret River.

Margaret River is a premium wine-growing area, set in beautiful rolling southwestern countryside, on a coast where mighty waves create world-class surfing and the geological structure has formed deep, spectacular limestone caves. With an early start, Mandurah on the Peel Inlet is a good coffee stop. Or go a little further, to where the massive Dawesville Cut joins the inlet and ocean, and pull over to take a look from **The Jolly Frog** restaurant (tel: 08-9534 4144).

The road to Bunbury is fast, and if you go scenic from here, the first town is Donnybrook. Named by Irish settlers in 1842, it was originally a timber town with convict-built roads. Farming holds sway now, and the area is famous for apples. Small shops and cafés might be open in each of the small towns you'll pass through, but Nannup will have the most choice. (The 'up' suffix to many Australian names is Aboriginal in origin, meaning 'water'.)

Next 'up' is Kirup, followed by Mullalyup and Balingup, where you turn off the main road onto the 251 for Nannup. The drive thus far is lovely; this part is idyllic, first winding along Balingup

Right: scenic Bunker Bay

Brook, then following the Blackwood River. Balingup/Nannup is 41km (25½ miles). Nannup (which means 'meeting place') is a picturesque small timber town with many original buildings. After a lunch stop at one of the cafés, take the secondary Mowen Road, via Quigup, to Margaret River, about 65km (40½ miles). This is a spectacular scenic route through forests, and it will take about an hour to reach your destination.

If you're travelling at the end of winter, check with local people about road conditions. Part of the road is unmade (compacted, but with no tarmac seal) and winter rains might have caused damage. If so, take the alternative Brockman Highway, also a very scenic drive.

Food and Lodgings

Make the most of your time by staying at one of the recommended bed-and-breakfast establishments, and go out for meals. **Crayfish Lodge** (tel: 08-9755 2028), at the corner of Caves Road and Canal Rocks Road, Yallingup , is close to the action. At Cowaramup, close to Margaret River, are **Old Bakehouse** (tel: 08-9755 5462) and **Noble Grape** (tel: 08-9755 5538). For information, call **Margaret River Visitor Centre**, corner Tunbridge Road and Bussell Highway (tel: 08-9757 2147; www.margaretriver.com).

Margaret River is full of restaurants and craft shops. But many wineries now have restaurants, so check with the Margaret River Visitor Centre. **Amberley** (tel: 08-9755 2288), **Brookland Valley** (tel: 08-9755 6042) and **Vasse Felix** (tel: 08-9756 5000) are recommended.

Right: limestone cave formations

Geological Wonders

The great thing about Margaret River is that if the weather deteriorates, you can go underground. More than 250 caves honeycomb the area, though only four can be visited. Caves Road is your route for **Mammoth Cave** and **Lake Cave** at Margaret River, **Jewel Cave** at Augusta, and **Yallingup Cave**. Lake Cave is like a huge ballroom entered by a winding staircase down into an immense crater, the reflected lights intensified by an underground lake. Mammoth Cave is very deep but easier to explore, with massive stalactite and delicate helictite formations, flowstone and 'shawls'. On display are fossils of prehistoric animals discovered here, including a Tasmanian Tiger.

An array of beaches are all accessible from Caves Road too. Surfing beaches – with names like Gallows, The Guillotine and Left-Hander – are so good that world championships are staged here. Yallingup beaches are also great for surfing and there's also a sheltered rock lagoon.

Vineyards

There are so many good vineyards in the region that you can't possibly visit them all. Here are some personal favourites. **Leeuwin**, Margaret River (tel: 08-9759 0000; www.leeuwinestate.com.au) is great, but expensive; also has alfresco food and a restaurant. **Amberley**, Yallingup (tel: 08-9755 2288; www.amberleyestate.com.au) also has a restaurant (lunch/dinner available) and a small art gallery. Others are **Evans and Tate**, Willyabrup (tel: 08-9755 6244; www.evansandtate.com.au); **Happ's**, Dunsborough (tel: 08-9755 3300; www.happs.com.au); and **Chateau Xanadu**, Margaret River (tel: 08-9757 2581; www.xanaduwines.com.au). If you wish to combine lunch with art, Brookland's **Flutes** restaurant (tel: 08-9755 6250) and its gallery of 'wine arts' would be an excellent choice.

Another change from wineries is **Bootleg Brewery**, Pusey Road, Willyabrup (tel: 08-9755 6300; www.bootlegbrewery.com.au), for a tasteful range of beers and lunch. En route to Perth, if there's daylight, make time to turn off the Bussell Highway about 7km (4 miles) past Busselton, at a big green sign for Tuart/Ludlow Fores – a 400-year-old forest of rare tuart trees. Instead of returning to Perth by freeway, stay with the coast road all the way into Fremantle.

Leisure Activities

SHOPPING

Central Perth has learned to try harder as the metropolis developed a satellite shopping style that makes everything available at the monster suburban sites. So city centre shopping offers attractions, specialist outlets and extra hours to tempt us.

Visitors will find a lot of what they need in the middle of Perth, especially characteristic Australian clothes, prestige items like diamonds and gold, and souvenirs (see *Itinerary 3* for some of the better quality 'Australiana' available in central Perth).

Other areas have their own style and specialities, especially Fremantle for arts and crafts, Claremont for fashion and lifestyle goods, and Guildford and others for antiques. More visitors are staying in self-catering accommodation, so I'll highlight the more interesting food and produce markets.

Central Perth retail hours are Monday to Thursday 9am–5.30pm, Friday 9am–9pm, Saturday 9am–5pm, and Sunday and public holidays noon–6pm.

Fashion

Perth's biggest department stores, **David Jones** and **Myer**, are both in Murray Street Mall (where the busker action can reach a crescendo). Both have wide fashion ranges, from current fad to classic, cosmetics and children's clothes. If time is short, they stock most everything that good department stores should.

Women's fashion shops in the arcades go from good and inexpensive **Katie's** and **Sussan**, to moderate **Brown Sugar** and **Portman**, to upmarket **Country Road**. As for men's clothes, Myer, Ahearn, and **Tony Barlow** in Hay Street are moderately priced; an expensive option is **Country Road**, at Forrest Chase, near Myer; while an inexpensive range is **Worth's** at Hay Street.

Australian-made leather shoes and boots for men are very good value, found at ordinary chain stores such as **Betts and Betts**, and **Perrini** and **Florsheim**. **Rivers** are mostly Aussie-made, Florsheim are guaranteed kangaroo leather, **Rossi** boots are really good value, and **Windsor Smith** use Australian leather in younger styles.

Rugged menswear figure large in the Australiana shops, such as **R M Williams** and **Outback Red**, but more can be found at the fascinating army surplus-style shops on Wellington Street, from Barrack Street to Pier Street. Hiking, camping and survival gear jostles with daggers, helmets and uniforms. Of these, only **The Stockade** breaks ranks, with country and western clothes. **Mountain Designs** at 862 Hay Street supplies professional-level outdoor clothing fit for climbing Mt Everest.

Then there's **Australian Geographic** at Forrest Chase and at Murray Street Mall, a shop that defies conventional description but is great for the unusual gifts – such as soundtrack CDs of frogs croaking, or rock crystals that replace deodorant.

Left: Forrest Chase shopping mall
Right: country clothes at The Stockade

Music

West Hay Street is a music enclave, with **Musgrove** at 900 Hay Street and **Clef** at 878 Hay Street specialising in instruments and sheet music. Nearby **78 Records** at 914 Hay Street has a good range of CDs. Classical music specialist **Wesley Classics** and the **Wesley CD Megastore** are in Wesley Arcade, which runs around the church connecting Hay and William streets. For alternative music, some local, venture upstairs at 142 William Street to **Complex Records**.

Collectors need to know about the massive stocks of second-hand items, including even wax cylinders let alone shellac 78s, held by **Bower Bird Records** at 284 Fitzgerald Street, North Perth. For enthusi-

asts, **Plastic Passion** at 43 Eighth Avenue, Maylands will also be worth a short trek.

Art-ful Shopping

Desert Designs at Fremantle High Street and Bayview Centre, Claremont, puts authentic Aboriginal designs on a range of goods from rugs to silks, and clothes for adults and kids. Also in Fremantle, **Hewitt's Art Bookshop** in High Street specialises in art, philosophy and cultural studies, while the **Fremantle Arts Centre Shop** at 1 Finnerty Street is crammed with all manner of ceramics, wood, glass, textiles and jewellery by WA artists.

Bellamy's Oceanic Art Galley and **Creative Native**, both along Fremantle's High Street stock a good collection of Aborigi-

nal crafts: digeridoos, spears, boomerangs, wooden jewellery, carvings and paintings. **Desert Designs Japinka Gallery**, 47 High Street, Fremantle, showcases the work of Aboriginal artist Jimmy Pike.

CraftWest at King Street Arts Centre, Murray Street specialises in contemporary arts with the usual ceramics and glass, and also jewellery worked in titanium, gold, silver and WA pearls and diamonds. The **Art Gallery of WA** shop at Perth Cultural Centre, James Street stocks books on art, architecture and gardening; catalogues of exhibitions; and cards, notepaper, posters, prints and gifts.

High-quality books on the natural, historic and cultural environment are the speciality of the **Western Australian Museum** shop, together with children's books, gifts, calendars and notepaper.

Claremont

A short train ride from Perth centre, Claremont is small and select with boutique shops, especially in **Old Theatre Lane**. Books, gifts, lingerie, fashion, shoes – and **Lady Kitchener's** cooks' shop are there. **That's Entertainment** specialises in swing and jazz recordings; **Zenith** has instruments, sheet music and more.

Opposite the Lane Bookshop is Cafécino coffee shop; nearby are designer clothes by Carla Zampatti and Liz Davenport. Indonesian and other ethnic furniture and collectables are at the **Shanghai Shed** nearby. Main shopping streets are **Bay View Terrace** – which is also the café strip, with the Red Rock Hotel – and **St Quentin Avenue**.

Antiques

Small collectibles and antiques figure strongly in **London Court**, but **Guildford's** shops have more variety, not by any means all fine, or even antique, but definitely interesting. Where else would you find a padded bag made for parachuting crockery and cutlery?

Nearer town, **Antique Importers of WA** and **Scurr Antiques** are at 768 and 769 Beaufort Street, respectively, at Mount Lawley. Antique, Victorian, Edwardian and 1920s furniture arrives from the UK by the container load.

Above: impressive collection of digeridoos, an Aboriginal instrument. **Top right:** choosing fruits in the market. **Right:** noisemakers at Subiaco Pavilion Markets

Markets

Fremantle Markets in South Terrace (Fri 9am–9pm, Sat 9am–5pm, Sun and holidays 10am–5pm) and **E-Shed Markets** (Fri, Sat, Sun and holidays 9am–6pm; Food Hall till 8pm) are best reached by train. The same goes for **Subiaco Pavilion Markets** (Thurs–Fri 10am–9pm, Sat, Sun and holidays 10am 5pm), corner Rokeby and Roberts roads, Subiaco, and **Station Street Markets**, over the railway from Pavilion (Fri, Sat, Sun and holidays 9am– 5.30pm).

The Subiaco Pavilion Markets has 55 speciality shops, including clothes, crafts, jewellery and pottery, and a food hall with inexpensive meals and live entertainment.

Station Street Markets is similar, with more character. Stallholders come and go, and their goods are more eclectic – Indonesian furniture, carpets, jewellery, books, gardening, old records and videos. An aisle of fresh fruit and vegetables is a big drawcard, with an open-air courtyard, central gazebo circled by cafés, and live entertainment spanning rock, pop and Hawaiian dancing.

Food Markets

If you stay in one of Perth's new apartment hotels, some gastronomic treats are in order. Fresh fruit and vegetables from Subiaco are hard to beat. These markets are much busier since a modern Subiaco station precinct, with a wide range of shops, restaurants and a supermarket, opened in 2000. The railway line which divided Subiaco has gone undergound, and all the new shops are within metres of the station.

If staying in Northbridge, basic produce and fish markets are at the corner of Roe and Fitzgerald streets. But across the tracks, **David Jones'** spectacular food hall in Murray Street Mall has everything, including ready-cooked gourmet treats. **Re Store**, Lake Street, Northbridge, is an Italian eye-opener, billed as a 'European Food Paradise'.

For Asian specialities go a little further north along William Street to **Prime Products**; or to **Capital Trading Co**, Forbes Road, Northbridge.

EATING OUT

Some Perth people with long memories remember when there were no restaurants. Nobody ate out, except in hotels. New migrants introduced their cultures and slowly Perth began to learn about food.

Given its brief history, Perth's gastronomic conversion is remarkable. Even a decade ago it was tough finding anything to eat in most suburbs after 9pm. Now there are cafés and restaurants – good ones – everywhere.

No longer a backwater, Perth is plugged into the network of western international cuisine that epitomises major cities all over the world. Today, chefs, managers and entrepreneurs work, study and spread their influence as they move around the world. National styles are filleted, adapted and stirred into the worldwide mix.

Experience and communications, greater mobility and low-cost travel, and demand from consumers have all been vital. Australian restauranteurs have always had the amazing resource of exceptional local produce, low-cost top quality meats, fish and game, and regional fruits and vegetables in cheap and copious supply. Now, they have the skills to turn these ingredients into fine food, and Perth's the richer for it.

So expect to eat well in Perth, in top hotels and restaurants, in the countless moderately priced places, and the cheap ones too. I have made a selection to cover most tastes and pockets. Good Western-style food can be anticipated in all, unless a specialist style is mentioned.

The price code guide below, in Australian dollars, is based on the approximate cost of a meal for two persons: $ = up to A$50; $$ = A$50–90; $$$ = over A$90. BYO means bring your own wine, beer, spirits. Most restaurants listed are licensed; ask if you can BYO.

On the Water

A reluctance to spoil the river and oceanside environment with development means Perth has limited opportunities to wine and dine with sea views. The places that are on the water make the most of their good fortune.

Blue Duck
151 Marine Parade, Cottesloe
Tel: 08-9385 2499; www.blueduck.com.au
Great beach views day and night. Innovative cuisine. $$

Indiana Tea Rooms
99 Marine Parade, Cottesloe
Tel: 08-9385 5005; www.indiana.com.au
Misleading name as the Indiana is open all day, and specialises in exotic Asian cuisine for Western palates. Built in grand style, with a tasteful pavilion. Located on a beach reserve in one of Perth's most prestigious areas. $$$

Jettys

Sorrento Quay, Hillary's Boat Harbour
Tel: 08-9448 9066; www.westshore.com.au
Smorgasbord as-much-as-you-want, including prawns, crayfish, etc. All indoors but located on oceanside jetty. $$

Jo-Jo's

Nedlands Jetty, end of Broadway, Nedlands
Tel: 08-9386 8757
Ten minutes by taxi from the city centre, this is a superior restaurant on the Swan, for lunch and dinner. Fresh seafood is Jo-Jo's speciality. $$$

Matilda Bay Restaurant

Hackett Drive, Crawley
Tel: 08-9423 5011; www.matbay.com.au
Riverside location by the University of WA; an elegant building with outstanding views that is matched by its first-rate imaginative menu. $$$

Moorings Café / On the Jetty

Barrack Street Jetty, Perth
Tel: 08-9325 4575
www.mooringscafe.com.au
Australian game and seafood is the speciality here; dine inside or on jetty. $$

Shun Fung

Barrack Street Jetty, Perth
Tel: 08-9221 1868; www.shunfung.com.au
Chinese seafood specialist, good Australian wine list; with private rooms for corporate and family groups. $$

Trigg Island Café

360 West Coast Highway, Trigg
Tel. 08-9447 0077
Not on an island or a highway, but overlooking the ocean close to Scarborough beach, this café has an innovative menu. $$

In Town

Anarkali Indian Restaurant

171 James Street, Northbridge
Tel: 08-9228 4464
Authentic Indian food with a high standard of service and presentation, Anarkali is the only Indian restaurant in Northbridge. Modern, tucked away from the hurly-burly of surrounding nightlife. $$

CBD

corner Hay and King streets, Perth
Tel: 08-9263 1859
Hotel restaurant with imaginative menu and good service; has pavement and in-restaurant dining. $$

C Restaurant Lounge

St Martin's Tower, 44 St Georges Terrace
Tel: 08-9220 8333
www.crestaurant.com.au
Revolving restaurant shows all of Perth, from ocean to hills, every 85 minutes. Pricey à la carte menu is excellent. Extensive wine list, good service and a luxurious ambience prove that not all feature restaurants rely on gimmicks. $$

Frasers Restaurant

Fraser Avenue, Kings Park
Tel: 08-9481 7100
www.frasersrestaurant.com.au
High-standard award-winning professional establishment worthy of its outstanding park location, with panoramic city and river views. $$$

James Street Kitchen

109 James Street, Northbridge
Tel: 08-9227 1437
Top value Chinese restaurant for seafood and fish; take head waiter's recommendation for fish special of the day. BYO. $

Left: located on an oceanside jetty, Jetty's seafood tastes even better
Above: Indiana Tea Rooms at Cottesloe Beach

King Street 44
44 King Street, Perth
Tel: 08-9321 4476
Brasserie-style, casual ambience, and a cuisine invigorated with Asian flavours. Excellent wine list too. $$

Maya Masala Indian Brasserie
49 Lake Street, Northbridge
Tel: 08-9328 5655
Authentic Indian food served casual café style. Very good value, but it's in the heart of a busy nightlife area which can be too raucous for outdoor dining. $

Old Shanghai
123 James Street, Northbridge
Tel: 08-9227 8633
Alfresco, covered food hall of Asian food specialists, from sushi to barbecue. Very inexpensive – substantial meals from as little as A$6. BYO, but one of the kiosks is a licensed bar. $

Picnicks Garden Restaurant
78-82 Outram Street, West Perth
Tel: 08-9481 6619
Creative modern Australian cuisine – an award-winning combination in recent years – served in this new location with terraced garden.$$

Simon's Seafood
73 Francis Street, Northbridge
Tel: 08-9227 9055; www.simons.com.au
Recommended, with especially good-value limited-choice lunch and dinner menus. BYO $$

Star Anise
225 Onslow Road, Shenton Park
Tel: 08-9381 9811; www.staraniseperth.com
Fine food restaurant that vies with Perth's best. Style is modern – Asian, French, Italian; it has no inhibitions. $$$

Yen Do
416 William Street, Northbridge
Tel: 08-9227 8833
Big, noisy and generally busy, with a predominance of Asian customers. Full range of Asian styles. Expect good value for your money here. BYO. $

Off-Centre

Alto's
424 Hay Street, Subiaco
Tel: 08-9382 3292
Dark glass and low lights contribute to this New York-style café, but Alto's has nothing to hide in its fine menu, served with friendly professionalism. Excellent for a night on the town. Good range of wines by glass as well as in bottle. $$

Café Di Rocco
531 Hay Street, Subiaco
Tel: 08-9388 6221
Authentic modern Italian menu by a proprietor/chef. Eat on the terrace or inside, lively atmosphere enhanced regularly by large family groups and well-supported by the local Italian community. The wood-fired pizza and hand-made pastas are specialities. Bread made in the pizza oven and good, low-price house wine are bonuses. $

Oriel Café And Brasserie
483 Hay Street, Subiaco
Tel: 08-9382 1886
The Mediterranean-style menu is perfect for this casual sidewalk restaurant. It's open 24 hours and the food is of a high standard. The bright young staff are eager to serve too. Meals can be small or extensive; good wines and atmosphere. $$

Above: in favour of Oriental flavour

Sails Seafood Restaurant
47 Mews Road, Fremantle
Tel: 08-9430 5151
www.sailrestaurant.com.au
Established by the same top catering professional who set up the Matilda Bay, this is a class act. Outside deck has views of Fishing Boat Harbour. $$

Surf Club
Port Beach Road, North Fremantle
Tel: 08-9430 6866
Eat outside under canvas by beach and sand dunes, or in the club-like interior. Good ranging menu. Also has a beach café. $$

In the Pub
You'd be hard pressed to find an old style Aussie pub in Perth. And why would you bother? They were watering holes with no time for niceties like food. Women who did venture in felt very uncomfortable. Liberated opening hours saw the end of the after-work swill. Competition and pressure from new generations have created a new kind of pub. Most have smartened up. Unfortunately, pubs remain the last retreat of die-hard smokers, which makes them no-go areas for many.

Brighter publicans have looked at the problem creatively, with indoor and outdoor food areas. Eating in the best pubs can now be a genuine pleasure. Good wine is available – but ask for a list, or bottled wine, unless you like the boxed version. Of course, beer lovers will find a far superior range, draught and bottled, than in any restaurant. Mostly open daily from around 11am to around midnight.

The Brass Monkey
corner of James and William streets, Northbridge
Tel: 08-9227 9596
Serves contemporary Australian food in a charismatic Victorian building. There are several bars, a courtyard and a good first-floor restaurant. Newest addition is the superb Grapeskin wine bar. $$

Queens Tavern
520 Beaufort Street, Highgate
Tel: 08-9328 7267
Courtyard or in-bar dining but be sure to see the interior, deliberately left 'unfinished'. $$

Above: Victorian-style Brass Monkey
Right: small talk over beer

NIGHTLIFE

Perth's nightlife ranges across the kind of fun you can find in most big cities – clubs, dancing, theatre, concerts and the rest. But there's a big bonus here. While in most parts of the world nightlife means a dive into dark recesses, often spiced with the heady aromas of smoke and booze, Perth takes a lot of its playtime out of doors. It's a claustrophobic's dream – to enjoy music, dinner and dancing, drama and even cinema under the clear night skies on a balmy summer's evening.

Cruises

Cruising the Swan at twilight, music playing, drink in hand and pleasant company all around is a great way to start an evening. There are a variety of cruises organised by **Captain Cook Cruises** (tel: 08-9325 3341; www.captaincookcruises.com.au) and all depart from the Barrack Street jetty. The **Seafood Dinner Cruise** provides live entertainment onboard an air-conditioned vessel. Departs at 7.30pm and returns 10.30pm; Wed and Fri–Sun. The **Dinner in the Valley** cruise goes out to the upper Swan Valley, with dinner and dancing ashore. Includes buffet dinner at a riverside restaurant, all wine, beer and soft drinks for the evening, plus live entertainment. Every Fri and Sat night 6pm–midnight from Nov–Dec. The **Evening Dinner Cruise** provides a buffet dinner, wine, beer and soft drinks. You can relax on the open deck and enjoy DJ sounds on the dance floor. Every Fri and Sat night from Oct–Apr 7–11.30pm. All cruises cost between A$70-80 per person.

Outdoor Cinema

Outdoor cinema is another treat only available in a Perth kind of summer. This is not drive-in movies, but deck-chair seating in garden settings, sometimes with catering and bar facilities. Current and classic films are screened, and ticket prices are similar to regular cinemas.

Camelot Outdoor Picture Garden
16 Lochee Street, Mosman Park
Tel: 08-9385 3827
www.lunapalace.com.au/camelot.htm
Probably the best of Perth's outdoor picture houses. Sit at the raised café and bar, or down on the lawn in a cypress-lined walled garden.

Kings Park
Fraser Avenue, off King's Park Road
Tel: 08-9480 3600; www.bgpa.wa.gov.au
The cinema is at the lakeside picnic area on May Drive; great for relaxed entertainment under the stars.

University of WA Somerville Auditorium
Stirling Highway entrance, Crawley
Tel: 08-9380 2691
www.theatres.uwa.edu.au
Lovely venue under the trees, ideal for your own picnic.

Outdoor Performances
Kings Park
Fraser Avenue, off King's Park Road
Tel: 08-9480 3600; www.bgpa.wa.gov.au
Kings Park is also the location for Shakespeare in the Park. Productions are generally

light-hearted, with a lot of audience involvement. Performances are usually held in the summer months of December and January. Take a rug or low chair, food and wine, and buy a ticket when you arrive. Check dates and prices with the park.

Quarry Amphitheatre
Corner of Oceanic Drive and Waldron Drive, City Beach
Tel: 08-9385 7144
www.quarryamphitheatre.com.au
Carved out of an abandoned limestone quarry, the Quarry Amphitheatre is another magical setting for theatre, concerts and ballet.

Spectator Sports

Western Australian Cricket Association (WACA)
Nelson Crescent, East Perth
Tel: 08-9265 7222; www.waca.com.au
Cricket under lights at the WACA is an experience that will never be available in the game's home, England. One-day matches start around 2pm and the evening session usually ends by 9.30pm.

Gloucester Park
Nelson Crescent, East Perth
Tel: 08-9323 3555
www.harness.org.au/wa/wata.htm
Western Australia's top trotting horse race track. Here you can dine and watch the horse-trotting races, and place a bet without leaving the table.

Indoor Theatre
Bookings are direct with the theatres, or through Ticketmaster (tel: 1300 136 166; www.ticketmaster7.com) or BOCS (tel: 08 9484 1133; www.bocsticketing.com.au). All kinds of theatre are available, from musical comedy to drama.

Effie Crump
81 Brisbane Street, Northbridge
Tel: 08-9227 7226; www.effiecrump.com
An intimate, quirky theatre with restaurant and bar; puts on several a year.

His Majesty's Theatre
825 Hay Street, Perth
Tel: 08-9484 1133

www.hismajestystheatre.com.au
Built in 1904, His Majesty's Theatre's horse-shoe-shaped auditorium is the venue for a range of productions.

Playhouse
3 Pier Street, Perth
Tel: 08-9231 2377
www.playhousetheatre.com.au
The Perth Theatre Company is based here.

Regal Theatre
474 Hay Street, Subiaco
Tel: 08-9484 1133
Another 'traditional' theatre that puts on a whole gamut of productions.

Subiaco Theatre Centre
180 Hammersley Road, Subiaco
Tel: 08-9381 3385
www.subiacotheatrecentre.com.au
Home to both Black Swan and Barking Gecko companies, with indoor and outdoor performances.

UWA's Theatres
University campus houses four very different theatres. They share the same website – www.theatres.uwa.edu.au (tel: 08-9380 2691): Dolphin Theatre, small (198-seat) studio venue with intimate ambience; **New Fortune Theatre**, Elizabethan styling with open-air stage and covered spectator galleries; **Octagon Theatre**, large (658 seats) general-purpose venue with thrust stage, seating on three sides; **Sunken Garden**, open-air setting used for innovative music and dance productions.

Cabaret and Live Performances

Burswood Dome
Great Eastern Highway, Burswood
Tel: 08-9362 7777
www.burswood.com.au
A popular venue for major concerts and sports.

Burswood Showroom
Great Eastern Highway, Burswood
Tel: 08-9362 7777
www.burswood.com.au
Live music and dinner nightly at the upscale Burswood Resort Hotel.

Left: watching a test match at the Western Australian Cricket Association

Downstairs at the Maj
835 Hay Street, Perth
Tel: 08-9321 5324
www.hismajestystheatre.com.au
Cabaret performances in cosy atmosphere.
Ticket price includes a light supper; bar and
table service provided.

Perth Concert Hall
5 St Georges Terrace, Perth
Tel: 08-9231 9900
www.perthconcerthall.com.au
Perth Concert Hall is home to the Western
Australian Symphony Orchestra and rightly
proud of the best acoustics of any auditorium on the continent.

PICA
(Perth Institute of Contemporary Art)
51 James Street, Perth
Tel: 08-9227 6144; www.pica.org.au
Performance arts as well as arts and media,
and a good call for up-to-date information
on the arts scene in general.

Music, Pubs and Clubs

Live music scene is big in Perth. Most pubs
have bands at weekends. Clubs come and
go, changing format often. Check the *West
Australian's Gig Guide* in the Friday paper
for current bands and locations. *Scoop* mag-
azine stays up-to-date on the club scene. Jaz-
zwa (tel: 08-9243 0401; www.jazzwa.com)
gives full data on jazz gigs and locations.

As well as Northbridge, many other areas
are lively after dark with a good club scene.
South of the tracks, Murray Street hosts some
of the best; to the north, Mount Lawley has
more; and going west you'll find entertainment in Leederville, Mount Claremont and
Fremantle.

Fly By Night Musicians' Club
Parry Street entrance, Fremantle
Tel: 08-9430 5976; www.flybynight.org
Has built a sound reputation for bringing in
top jazz and blues acts.

Luxe Bar
446 Beaufort Street, Mount Lawley
Tel: 08-9228 9690
Classy and comfortable newcomer, excellent
service, modern/jazz sounds. Cool, overseas
visiting musicians such as *Kinobe* drop in.

Metro City
146 Roe Street, Northbridge
Tel: 08-9228 0500; www.metros.com.au
Spectacular and worth a look just for the
building and interior design. It's a dance club
that also showcases top performing bands.

Westend
Centre King/Murray Streets, Perth
Tel: 08-9321 4094
Belgian beer café, imported beers and wide
wine list complementing speciality foods.

Jazz Venues
Hyde Park Hotel
www.hydeparkhotel.com.au
Leading music venue, hosting the Perth Jazz
Society (www.perthjazzsociety.com) and
Jazz Club of WA.

Norfolk Hotel
47 South Terrace, Fremantle
Tel: 08-9335 5405
Another jazz favourite.

Melbourne Hotel
Centre Hay/Milligan Streets
Tel: 08-9320 3333

Above: chill out to some sexy jazz sounds

CALENDAR OF EVENTS

Book early for special events in December, January and February, the long school holiday period. Many Perth people quit the city during the holidays, but country kids and their families fill the gap, especially after Christmas, when good weather is virtually guaranteed.

January – February

Perth Cup: WA's premier horse race at Ascot for the A$250,000 Healthway Cup; held on January 1.

Hopman Cup: Unique, prestigious international invitation tennis, with mixed pairs representing their nation.

Fremantle Sardine Festival: Entertainment on the Esplanade around the main attraction, freshly caught Fremantle sardines.

Skyworks: Fireworks to music in a massive skyshow, Perth's biggest outdoor event that draws 350,000 spectators to the riverside.

Australia Day Racenight: Live bands and fireworks at the Gloucester Park 'trots' – WA's premier trotting horse race track.

Heineken Classic: Million-dollar-plus international golf tournament, an Australian PGA event.

Perth Grand Prix: High point of the track and field season, featuring international athletes plus the best from across Australia.

Festival of Perth: Feb–Mar, biggest international arts festival in southern hemisphere.

March – August

Rottnest Festival: 4 days of family fun and special events on the island.

Avon Descent: White-water classic, 2-day event with 600 craft racing a 133km (83 miles) course from Northam to Perth.

City to Surf: 10,000 runners, walkers and wheelchair riders contest a hilly 12km (8 miles) course from St Georges Terrace to the Indian Ocean at City Beach, or a short 4km (2½ miles) course from Perry Lakes to City Beach.

September – October

Kings Park Wildflower Festival: Natural displays of wildflowers and hundreds of potted specimens make this event Australia's largest and most varied native and wildflower exhibition.

Right: an outdoor jazz festival

Artrage Festival: Alternative arts take to the streets; indoor theatre also staged, with drama, dance, comedy and cabaret.

Perth Royal Show: Began as an agricultural/horticultural show, now includes general entertainment and sideshows as well as sheep shearing, wood chopping, etc.

Spring in the Valley: Weekend of wine, food, music and art at Swan Valley wineries and other locations.

Gay Pride March: Gay and lesbian extravaganza through the streets of Northbridge.

Rally Australia: 4-day round of the FIA World Championship, from October–November, including time trials on specially constructed track at Langley Park in city.

November – December

Test Match: Spanning November–March, Australia versus the season's international touring team (England or West Indies draws the biggest crowds) at the Western Australian Cricket Association (WACA). Five or six tests may be played each season. Perth usually hosts the first or last of them.

Ascot Summer Carnival: Biggest horse racing event of the year, culminating in the Perth Cup on 1 January.

Shakespeare in the Park: Open-air bring your own supper romp in Kings Park, running through to January.

Practical Information

GETTING THERE

By Air

Around a dozen international airlines serve Perth, all handled in Western Australia by Qantas (tel: 131 313; www.qantas.com.au). Direct international flights come from parts of Asia, Africa, Europe and the Pacific region. Domestic flights by Qantas and Virgin Blue (tel: 136 789; www.virginblue.com.au) connect Australian destinations.

Domestic and international terminals are east of the city and 10km (6 miles) apart by road. From central Perth, allow 40 minutes to reach the domestic terminal, and 15 minutes more for the international terminal.

Getting to the city: The main taxi companies are Black and White (tel: 131 008) and Swan (tel: 131 330). The fare to central Perth – located some 20km (12.5 miles) northeast – should be A$15–20. Car hire firms at the airport are Avis, Budget, Delta Europe, Hertz, National and Thrifty. An airport shuttle service by Feature Tours runs to the city and between terminals..

By Rail

The Indian Pacific links Perth twice weekly with the eastern states of Australia. The journey from Sydney via Adelaide takes 3 nights (64 hours). Options are first-class or economy sleeper, and economy seat. Contact Great Southern Railway (tel: 132 147; www.gsr.com.au) for fares and details. Indian Pacific and all country rail services arrive at the East Perth terminus, a 5-minute taxi ride from the city centre.

By Road

A daily coach service links Perth with Adelaide, South Australia and the north. The joint operators are Greyhound Pioneer (tel: 132 030; www.greyhound.com.au) and McCaffertys (tel: 132 030; www.mccaffertys.com.au) All services terminate at Wellington Street in the city centre.

Left: Perth Railway Station
Right: kangaroo express

By Sea

Cruise ships arrive at Fremantle, 20km (12 miles) downriver from Perth.

TRAVEL ESSENTIALS

When to Visit

All year is good, and autumn (March–May) is best, when temperatures fall lower and the cooling sea breeze that's so welcome in summer eases off. The moderate mediterranean-style climate means the weather shouldn't deter you any time of the year, though. The low humidity means that high-20s temperatures are very comfortable in Perth.

A year-long tourist season eases the pressure of numbers, so you can plan to visit for special events, such as the Festival of Perth (February/March), without accommodation problems.

Weather

Perth's mediterranean-style climate gives distinctive seasons, with sunshine all year and some rain in winter and spring. The city is often totally dry for months on end and summer can be very hot, with temperatures in

the high 30s°C (86°F). Average temperatures are: winter (June–August) 18°C (65°F); spring (September–November) 22°C (72°F); summer (December–February) 30°C (86°F); and autumn (March–May) 24°C (75°F).

Visas and Passports

All visitors need passports and visas, except New Zealanders (passports only). Australian arrangements with many countries mean that 80 percent of visitors now arrive on ETAs (electronic travel authority) issued by a travel agent or airline. There's no immigration department charge for ETAs. They are valid for a year, but you can stay only three months per trip. Visitors wanting to extend their stay without leaving Australia may be able to do so by contacting the Immigration Department, 45 Francis Street, Northbridge, Perth (tel: 131 881). If your home country has no Australian ETA arrangement, contact the Australian Embassy office there. Visas are issued according to personal circumstances.

Customs

The duty-free allowance for adults over 18 years is: A$400 of dutiable gifts; 1.125 litres of alcohol; and 250g of tobacco products. If you're under 18, the allowance is A$200 of gifts, and no alcohol or tobacco. Strict regulations apply to the importation of food, plants, animals and by-products. Assume that these items will be confiscated by Customs officers. Drug smuggling of any kind carries heavy penalties.

There's no limit on the amount of cash you can carry in or out of the country, but any more than A$10,000 cash or its foreign currency equivalent must be reported to Customs. You can bring 3 months' supply of prescription medication into Australia, but it may be useful to carry a doctor's certificate and explanatory letter.

Quarantine

All animals, including seeing-eye dogs, entering the country are subject to a minimum 6-months quarantine. However, regular travellers with such dogs can make prior certification arrangements in their home countries.

Vaccinations

If you are arriving from areas affected by yellow fever or outbreaks of other infectious diseases, it is advisable to have documentary proof of vaccination.

Clothing

Lightweight is best most of the year, with a few layers that will mix and match. Even in winter one good sweater will be sufficient, plus a folding umbrella. Top coats are rarely seen in Perth. Informality is the general rule and you'll be comfortable in casual clothes just about everywhere. Hats and sunglasses are advisable; the sun is fierce.

Ties and jackets are hardly ever worn except in business situations. In top hotels and restaurants you might feel more comfortable with one or the other so the staff don't outdo you.

Electricity

Current is rated at 230–250 volts, 50 hertz. Standard plugs have three flat pins, and you may need an adaptor for heavier use appliances such as hairdryers. Universal outlets for 110 volts shavers, etc are found in most accommodations; otherwise, a transformer and adaptor is necessary.

Time Differences

All of Western Australia, including Perth, is 8 hours in advance of Greenwich Mean Time. Australia's eastern states are 1½–2 hours ahead of Perth. Because they operate a daylight saving system, and WA does not, the eastern states are 2½–3 hours ahead between October and March.

Left: casual and comfortable

practical information

GETTING ACQUAINTED

Geography

Perth is the most isolated capital city on earth, separated by thousands of kilometres of desert and bush from other Australian capitals. Its location is the south-west corner of Western Australia, which is the country's largest state, covering 2.5 million sq km (1 million sq miles) and one-third of the continent. WA is 10 times the size of the UK, almost as big as India. But the population is just 1.8 million, with 1.3 million living in the Perth metropolis. Greater Perth spreads 80km (49¾ miles) north to south and another 65km (40½ miles) west to east, from the Indian Ocean to the Darling Ranges. The Swan River runs through the heart of Perth, linking it to the port city of Fremantle.

Government and Economy

Australia has three government levels – local, state and federal, with compulsory voting for the state and federal governments. Both are based on the Westminster, two-house system combined with proportional representation (PR). One outcome of PR voting is that minor parties in the Senate can stymie the federal government in the House of Representatives. Compromise is often necessary to ease government policies through the upper house. State governments have considerable power too. The result can be a different approach and different laws, state by state.

Local governments (of cities, towns or shires) deal with most of the day-to-day civic needs of the population. In WA, there are no party politics in local government. Though a tiny proportion of its people live outside the cities, mining and agriculture continue as the major export earners of WA. Mining of everything from mineral sands to gold and diamonds is a bedrock industry, producing almost 75 percent of exports. Agriculture is next, with about 20 percent, followed by manufacturing, forestry and fishing. Although many jobs depend on these activities, most people are city dwellers working at the same kinds of jobs as city dwellers all over the civilized world. Recent growth industries for Perth and WA include tourism, high technology, tertiary education and wine production.

Population

The population grew fast after gold was discovered in the 1890s. Newcomers were virtually all from the British Isles, though some 't'othersiders' came via the eastern states. Ethnically mixed migration increased greatly after World War II and Perth's multi-cultural society at the end of this century is a marked contrast with that of 1900. WA has many second or third generations of migrant families, but one-third of today's population of 1.8 million were born overseas. Ireland and the UK remain the source of more migrants than any other area, though total European and Asian migration has increased.

MONEY MATTERS

Currency

The Australian dollar is the local currency. Coin denominations are 5, 10, 20 and 50 cents, $1 and $2. Notes are $5, $10, $50 and $100. There is no limit on cash brought into or taken from Australia (but see *Customs* section regarding declaration).

Foreign Exchange

Banks operate Mon to Thurs 9.30am–4pm, and Fri 9.30am–5pm. Some hotels will exchange major currencies for guests, and there's a 24-hour agency at the airport.

Travellers Cheques

International travellers cheques will be cashed at major establishments such as airports, banks, hotels, motels. Thomas Cook has several city branches; the major one is in Hay Street Mall (Mon to Fri 8.30am–5.30pm, Sat 10am–2pm). American Express is also in Hay Street Mall. Fees and rates of exchange may vary between establishments.

The WA Visitors Centre, Albert Facey

Above: Western Australia flag

House, Forrest Chase (tel: 1300 361 351) is open every day and will exchange all major travellers' cheques and currency. Opening hours are as follows: Mon to Thurs 8.30am–6pm, Fri 8.30am–7pm, Sat 8.30am–5pm, Sun 10am–5pm.

It's advisable to change your money before heading out of Perth or Fremantle – banks are few in country WA.

Credit Cards

Best-known international cards are listed here, with local numbers to call in case of problems.
American Express (tel: 1800 222 000)
Diners Club (tel: 1300 360 060)
MasterCard (tel: 1800 120 113)
Visa (tel: 1800 801 256)

Pricing

A general sales tax was introduced in July 2000, replacing wholesale and other taxes.

Departure Tax

This is now included in the ticket price.

Tipping

Tipping is not obligatory in Australia, and isn't expected in Perth restaurants, taxis, etc. However, if you have had specially good service and wish to tip, you will not offend.

GETTING AROUND

Buses

Transperth (www.transperth.wa.gov.au; InfoLine, tel: 136 213) runs the city bus, train and ferry services. Pay as you board buses; train and ferry tickets are available from self-service machines at stations and jetties.

Central city bus travel is free, on the regular buses and CATS (Central Area Transit). Apart from the afternoon rush hour, traffic

jams are few and buses plentiful, so this is a good way to cruise around town. The free zone covers most of the inner area visitors will want to see, from Kings Park to the Causeway, and east to Newcastle Street. Blue or red CATS are distinctive buses serving a couple of big inner-city loops, from the Swan through Northbridge, and west Perth to the WACA ground in east Perth.

The bus service out of town is mostly radial, which is pretty good for tourists heading out and back (to Fremantle, etc); it's less useful for inter-suburb links.

Trains

A modern electric air-conditioned train system runs through Perth to Fremantle in the south and Joondalup, north. It's a very good way to travel during the day, but with far fewer passengers on the trains at night, security problems have developed. Although incidents are few and far between, and security guards are employed, you are advised against using trains late at night.

Ferries

Transperth, the city's bus authority, runs the only ferry across the Swan – from the city to south Perth. Despite ever-increasing road traffic, other attempts to float commuter ferry services have failed.

Perth to Fremantle trips are available from Captain Cook Cruises, one-way or return (tel: 08-9325 3341, daily 9.45am, 11am, 2.45pm.) Cost of the one-way journey is A$15.

Taxis

Most cabs are modern, white, Ford or Holden. You can hail them on the street, find them at taxi ranks, or phone Black and White (tel: 131 008) and Swan (tel: 131 330). If you should encounter any problems, note driver and cab details, and call the company.

Rates are reasonable – A$1.17 per km and flagfall A$2.90 (day), A$4.20 (night, weekends and public holidays.) If you're part of a large group, these companies also operate people-movers than can take six or more passengers. People-mover rates are A$1.74 per km and flagfall A$4.20.

For extended journeys, or tours, sedans are available at A$50.60 per hour, and people-movers at A$52 per hour.

Left: travel in style

HOURS AND HOLIDAYS

Business Hours

Central retail hours are Mon to Thurs 9am–5.30pm; Fri 9am–9pm; Sat 9am–5pm; and Sun and public holidays noon–6pm.

Small businesses such as restaurants, snack bars and local corner shops (often called delis) open according to demand, often until late at night and through the weekend.

Bank hours are Mon to Thurs 9.30am–4pm; Fri 9.30am–5pm. Most businesses close at the weekend.

Public Holidays

New Year's Day	1 January
Australia Day	26 January
Anzac Day	25 April
Good Friday	March/April
Easter Monday	March/April
Foundation Day	5 June
Queen's Birthday	2 October
Labour Day	6 March
Christmas Day	25 December
Boxing Day	26 December
New Year's Eve	31 December

ACCOMMODATION

Central Perth is compact and has a wide range of hotels, apartment hotels and hostels at or near the centre of town. The most expensive are still reasonable compared to sim-

ilar quality accommodation in other Australian cities. Hotels in this category are all luxuriously appointed, with air-conditioning, in-house movies, and often Internet data points in rooms. Attentive service and a range of restaurants, bars and extra facilities should be expected. Check for seasonal and other special rates.

Some of the smaller hotels have large rooms that can be shared by a small family, and are very good value. Another option are hotel apartments; several of these high-quality developments are now offering an alternative to hotel accommodation in Perth, even for single-night bookings. Hostels too are plentiful, in keeping with the growing number of people backpacking in Australia. Most accommodation listed here is close to the city centre.

Bookings

The WA Visitor Centre (tel: 1300 361 351) is the agent for most hotels and will help with all enquiries.

Price categories (for a standard double room, in Australian dollars): $ = A$85–120; $$ = A$120–200; $$$ = A$200–300.

Expensive

Burswood International Resort Casino
Great Eastern Highway, Burswood, Perth
Tel: 08-9362 7777; Fax: 08-9470 2553
www.burswood.com.au
Hotel and entertainment centre on Swan

Above: eclectic sculptures at the Burswood International Resort Casino

River, with casino, tennis centre, golf, show-room and sports dome; as well as all antic-ipated luxury hotel features. Wide range of room and suite rates; check for special pack-ages. $$$

Crowne Plaza Perth
54 Terrace Road, Perth
Tel: 08-9325 3811; Fax: 08-9221 1564
www.crowneplaza.com
Between CBD and riverside, some rooms with river views. Close to shopping, enter-tainment and cultural centres. $$$

Duxton
1 St Georges Terrace, Perth
Tel: 08-9261 8000; Fax: 08-9261 8020
www.duxton.com
Top-end establishment with large facilities aimed at business use, conferences and con-ventions; luxurious rooms with river views, full range of services. $$$

Parmelia Hilton
14 Mill Street, Perth
Tel: 08-9215 2000; Fax: 08-9215 2001
www.hilton.com
Central location, off St Georges Terrace, near Kings Park and river, with heated pool, sauna, restaurant, wine bar, night club. $$$

Rendezvous Observation City
The Esplanade, Scarborough Beach
Tel: 08-9245 1000; Fax: 08-9245 1345
www.rendezvoushotels.com
On major surfing beach, all rooms with bal-cony and sea view, 15 minutes from central Perth. $$$

The Sebel Of Perth
37 Pier Street, Perth
Tel: 08-9325 7655; Fax: 08-9325 7383
www.mirvachotels.com.au

Boutique-style with extra-large rooms, non-smoking floors, health club and all top ho-tel services. Heated outdoor pool in a garden setting. $$$

Moderate

Criterion Hotel
560 Hay Street, Perth
Tel: 08-9325 5155; Fax: 08-9325 4176
www.criterion-hotel-perth.com.au
Striking art deco exterior marks this well-re-stored small hotel directly opposite the Town Hall. Room price includes breakfast. $$

Goodearth Hotel
195 Adelaide Terrace, Perth
Tel: 08-9492 7777; Fax: 08-9221 1956
e-mail: stay@goodearthhotel.com.au
Walking distance from attractions and free inner-city bus stops outside. Accommoda-tion ranging from studio apartments to two-bedroom family units, each with kitchenette, TV, phone. Restaurant with river view, park-ing. $$

Holiday Inn
778 Hay Street, Perth
Tel: 08-9261 7200; Fax: 08-9261 7277
www.perth-cityctr.holiday-inn.com
Reliable international style with all facilities, and in the heart of the city, within walking distance of shops and entertainment. $$

Hotel Ibis
334 Murray Street, Perth
Tel: 08-9322 2844; Fax: 08-9321 6314
www.accorhotels.com.au
Near entertainment and cultural centres, 15 minutes walk from Kings Park, with bar, restaurant and bistro. $$

Kings Perth Hotel
517 Hay Street, Perth
Tel: 08-9325 6555; Fax: 08-9221 1539
www.kingshotel.com.au
Central location, with restaurant, bar, pool, parking. $$

Mercure Hotel
10 Irwin Street, Perth
Tel: 08-9326 7000; Fax: 08-9221 3344
www.accorhotels.com.au
Central for CBD, shopping and entertain-

Above: art deco style Criterion Hotel

ment, with pool, sauna, gym, restaurants, bar and valet parking service. $$

Miss Maud Swedish Hotel
97 Murray Street, Perth
Tel: 08-9325 3900; Fax: 08-9221 3225
www.missmaud.com.au
Charismatic and quirky exterior makes this building stand out. All central attractions nearby; hotel is an airport/day tour stop. Miss Maud (real person) has a small chain of pastry, coffee and lunch restaurants, including one at this small hotel. Room price includes smorgasbord breakfast. $$

Novotel Langley Perth Hotel
corner Adelaide Terrace and Hill Street Perth
Tel: 08-9221 1200; Fax: 08-9221 1669
www.accorhotels.com.au
Equidistant from river, jetty and centre, all a short walk away. Features Fenian's Irish Pub as well restaurant, gym, sauna and sundeck. $$

Vines Resort
Verdelho Drive, WA 6069
Tel: 08-9297 0700; Fax: 08-9297 3333
www.vines.com.au
Its 27-hole golf course (rated the No 2 resort course in Australia) warrants the Vines' inclusion here, even though it's 45 minutes from Perth in the Swan Valley wine-growing area. $$

Inexpensive
Ambassador Hotel
196 Adelaide Terrace, Perth
Tel: 08-9325 1455; Fax: 08-9325 1455
e-mail: reserve@ambassador-hotel.com.au
Good location for river, entertainment/shopping areas, all rooms with TV, tea/coffee, fridge, phone, etc. $

Emerald Hotel
24 Mount Street, Perth
Tel: 08-9481 0866; Fax: 08-9321 4789
e-mail: stay@emeraldhotel.com.au
A family-run boutique hotel, all rooms with mini-kitchen and TV; two-bedroom apartments also available. Gym, sauna and spa; restaurant for breakfast and dinner. Location is close to Kings Park. $

Right: backpackers' prayers answered

Sullivans Hotel
166 Mounts Bay Road, Perth
Tel: 08-9321 8022; Fax: 08-9481 6762
www.sullivans.com.au
Between Kings Park and river, only 5 minutes from city centre and offering free shuttle service. Pool, gardens, café, parking, free guest bicycles. Rooms (including 2-bedroom apartments) are air-conditioned, with TV, coffee, phones, etc; extremely good value. $

Hotel Apartments
Broadwater Como Resort
137 Melville Parade, Como
Tel: 08-9474 4222; Fax: 08-9474 4216
www.broadwaters.com.au
Close to river south side, shopping centre, restaurants, cinema; 4km from CBD. Aircon, full kitchen, laundry, phone/fax, TV/video. Pool, spa, sauna, tennis and licensed Como Beach Café. $$

Mountway Holiday Apartments
36 Mount Street, Perth
Tel: 08-9321 8307
e-mail: info@mountwayunits.com.au
Excellent budget-priced, secure apartments well-equipped with kitchen and bath. Centrally located for city and Kings Park. $

Quest on James
228 James Street, Northbridge
Tel: 08-9227 2888; Fax: 08-9227 2800
www.questwa.com.au
In Northbridge, Perth's nightlife area, its two or three-bed apartments are equipped with kitchen, laundry, lounge/dining room, aircon, TV, phone, etc. Has parking, pool, spa, barbecues and restaurant. $$

Hostels and Backpackers

Cost of a single room in a hostel is generally below A$50 per night. Backpackers are much cheaper, at around A$20 a night.

Aberdeen Lodge
79 Aberdeen Street, Northbridge
Tel: 08-9227 6137; Fax: 08-9387 2892
Centrally-located; shared facilities.

Backpackers International
Lake/Aberdeen Street, Northbridge
Tel: 08-9227 9977; Fax: 08-9385 3180
In the middle of the nightlife area; has single and twin rooms; kitchen and laundry facilities, linen supplied.

City Holiday Apartments
537 William Street, Mt Lawley
Tel: 08-9227 1112; Fax: 08-9227 1889
www.cityapartments.com
Apartments are 10 minutes' walk from city centre, on main bus route. Cooking facilities, laundry, linen, TV, etc, parking.

Jewel House YMCA
180 Goderich Street, Perth
Tel: 08-9325 8488; Fax: 08-9221 4694
www.ymcajewelhouse.com
Has single, double and family rooms, restaurant serving low-cost breakfast and dinner.

Murray Street Backpackers Hostel
119 Murray Street, Perth
Tel: 08-9325 7627; Fax: 08-9221 0083
www.murrayst.com
Another central establishment that provides shared cooking facilities.

Youth Hostels Association
253 William Street, Northbridge
Tel: 08-9328 6121; Fax: 08-9227 9784
www.yha.com.au
Backpacker establishment in Northbridge.

EMERGENCIES

Useful numbers
Dial 000, only in an emergency needing police, ambulance or fire brigade. For police attendance, call 9222 1111. Otherwise, the number for local police stations is 13 1444.

Security and Crime
Perth is a relatively safe place with no special problems, but normal city precautions are always advisable. A taxi is probably the best way to move around late at night, unless you're walking a short distance on busier, well-lit streets. Lock doors, don't leave valuables or bags on display in parked cars. Don't carry more cash than you need; use hotel deposit boxes.

Medical
Emergency number: 1800 022 222. This is a free 24-hour service.

Medical services are good and a wide range of doctors, specialist services (such as physiotherapy) and hospitals are readily available in Perth. Most travellers are ineligible for free treatment, so it is wise to carry health and accident insurance. The basic cost of a medical consultation is A$35.

Reciprocal agreements are in place with Finland, Italy, Malta, the Netherlands, New Zealand, Sweden and the UK. Passport holders of these countries can reclaim the cost of medical treatment from Medicare in Australia.

Pharmacies
Also known as 'chemists', pharmacies are run by qualified professionals who dispense prescribed medication. They also sell non-prescription medication, plus toiletries, cosmetics, film, etc. Visitors can bring up to 3 months' supply of prescription medication into Australia. Carry a doctor's certificate and letter explaining what you need, to avoid problems with Customs.

Beaufort Street Pharmacy, 647 Beaufort Street (tel: 08-9328 7775) opens 24 hours, 7 days a week. Others open until 9pm or midnight: check the *Yellow Pages* for the most convenient outlet.

Dental
Many dentists practise in the city centre or nearby. During business hours find a convenient surgery, listed in the *Yellow Pages* under dentists. For emergency treatment go to Lifecare Dental (tel: 08-9221 2777), 425 Wellington Street (adjacent to Myers store). Otherwise, call any hospital accident and emergency department.

Drinking Water

Tap water is safe to drink in Australian cities. Bottled mineral water is widely available.

Sunburn

The Australian sun is particularly harsh. As a result, the 'suntanned Aussie' image is fading fast as more people automatically use sunblock every day. Wide-brimmed hats or caps, and sunglasses, are essential for comfort and protection most of the year. If you are fair-skinned and/or unused to strong sunshine, but do want to sunbathe, do so in the morning or late afternoon.

COMMUNICATIONS AND NEWS

Postal

Post offices are open Mon to Fri 9am–5pm, and the central post office in Forrest Chase also opens Sat 9am–12.30pm; and Sun noon–4pm. Forrest Chase office will hold mail for visitors for up to a month. American Express in Hay Street Mall also offers this service to its cardholders.

Telephone and Fax

Local calls from public phones cost 40 cents, with no time limit. Long-distance calls in Australia and to other countries can be made from most phones, including public phones and hotels. Some public phones operate by card, available from post offices and large newsagents. Competition is driving rates down and special offers are being introduced continuously. In general, long-distance calls are cheaper later in the day. For rates call Telstra on 132 200.

The country code for Australia is 61; the area code for Perth is 08. If calling from overseas and within Perth, drop the prefix 0. Six digit numbers starting with 13 and toll-free 1300 and 1800 numbers can only be dialled within Australia.

For overseas phone calls, the access code is 0011, followed by the country code and number. For overseas faxes, the access code is 0015. Overseas country codes are all listed at the back of the telephone directory.

Fax machines are available at international-class hotels, post offices and other locations. Short- or long-term mobile phone rentals are available. Vodarent will deliver to your hotel. Call 1800 24 5001 for details.

Media

ABC (Australian Broadcasting Corporation) is best for up-to-the minute news. The national broadcast TV is channel 2; national radio, FM 97.7 and AM 810 and AM 585; local radio, AM 720. Tourist information radio is on FM 87.6. SBS (Special Broadcasting Service) national TV carries foreign language news early in the morning; local community Channel 31 has BBC news every evening and is also strong on local events, tourist information, restaurant reviews, etc.

The *West Australian* is Perth's only daily newspaper, Mon–Sat. The Saturday issue is a bumper. The *Sunday Times* is the only Sunday paper. *The Australian* is a national paper, printed in Perth and available Mon–Sat. Weekly news magazines include the *Bulletin* and *Time*. In central Perth, airmail editions and other language newspapers may be found at the State Library in the Cultural Centre, and on sale at the Plaza Newsagency, in Plaza Arcade. Free local weekly newspapers abound. Most useful are likely to be entertainment oriented tabloids like *Hype*, *Zebra* and *X-Press* found at most music stores. *Scoop* is a good, on-sale, Perth glossy mag covering lifestyle and entertainment.

USEFUL INFORMATION

Disabled People

WA is setting the pace for Australia, with its advanced policies. Building codes require all new constructions to be accessible. In

Left: calling home

general, advance notice and details of your disability will ensure best service, especially from airlines, hotels, restaurants and other venues. In Perth, the Disability Commission (tel: 08-9426 9200) will advise.

Taxis: Request a multi-purpose taxi from the cab companies Black and White, and Swan. Rates should be the same as for regular taxis.

Smoking

WA is advanced in its anti-smoking campaign and most people would expect you to ask first before lighting up. Smoking is not allowed in public venues and transport. The Healthway Quit campaign has even resulted in open-air sports stadia such as the WACA banning smoking. Legislation has put a legal smoking ban on restaurants and other places serving food indoors. Pubs remain a grey area; some allow smoking so please check beforehand.

SPORTS

Sport has a high profile in Australia. In Perth you have access to most, though snow skiers will be disappointed. Water skiing is an alternative, perhaps. Some major interests are listed below. Call the Ministry of Sport (tel: 08-9387 9700; www.dsr.wa.gov.au) for extra information.

Aerobics

Fitness centres and gyms are everywhere, offering a range of classes and services. See the *Yellow Pages*.

Cricket

Headquarters of the sport in WA is the WACA stadium on Wellington Street, just east of the city centre. The season runs from October to March. International and domestic 1-day matches are very popular, especially the day/night variety played under lights at the WACA. Sheffield Shield is the inter-state contest, with matches scheduled for 4 days. Five-day Test matches are still the pinnacle of the sport and Perth hosts one every season. Call the WACA (tel: 08-9265 7222; www.waca.com.au) for details of fixtures.

Football

Australian Rules football ('footy') is the most popular sport in Australia. WA has two teams in the national competition, the Eagles and the Dockers. In the March to September season their matches are usually played at Subiaco Oval, and club sides play at grounds all around Perth.

Golf

Public courses are plentiful, the closest being Burswood Park, just over the Causeway on Great Eastern Highway. In the western suburbs are Wembley, Lake Claremont, Fremantle and Point Walter.

Horse Racing

This sport is very popular in Australia. Perth has racing through the year, at the Belmont or Ascot tracks, both a few minutes' taxi ride from the city centre. The facilities are superb. The Summer Carnival meeting at Ascot, beginning around 11 December and climaxing with Perth Cup Day on 1 January, is a fashion

highlight of the year. Racing is on every weekend and many weekdays and the cost of entry is very low, giving access to all areas except the upper part of the members' stand. Even non-gamblers will enjoy Perth's races.

Running and Jogging

Running is popular and safe in Perth. A 10-km (6-mile) circuit around the bridges is well-used; Kings Park is perfect for off-road running on trails or grass. To run in friendly company, call WAVAC (WA Veterans AC; tel: 08-9330 3803). They have a running and walking event every Sunday morning at different locations around the city, a Tuesday night Kings Park training group, and track and field meetings from October to March.

Surf Carnivals

Surf lifesavers from Western Australia's 20 clubs watch the beaches to make swimming safe through the summer season. The carnivals are competitive events where they test their skills in the water, on surf-skis and in surf-boats, and on the sand in sprints and 'flags'. A variety of events, from junior competition through iron man contests, up to the full club carnivals, occur from October to March. Call the Surf Life Saving Association (tel: 08-9244 1222; www.slswa.asa.au) for dates, beach locations and details.

Yacht Racing

Club events and championships are held on the Swan's Melville Water, and the season is from October to April. Twilight sailing presents a more sociable, less competitive opportunity to get on the water. Crew members are always needed, calling any of the clubs listed in the *Yellow Pages*.

USEFUL ADDRESSES

Tourism Office

Western Australian Visitor Centre, Albert Facey House, Forrest Place, corner Wellington Street, Perth, tel: 1300 361 351; www.westernaustralia.net.
Open Mon–Thurs 8.30am–6pm, Fri 8.30am–7pm, Sat 8.30am–5pm, and Sun 10am–5pm. This should be your first port of call for all tourism and travel related enquiries.

Airline Offices

Air New Zealand: 44 St Georges Terrace, tel: 08-9221 1925; www.airnz.com.au.
British Airways: 77 St Georges Terrace, tel: 08-9425 5333; www.britishairways.com.au.
Cathay Pacific: 40 The Esplanade, tel: 08-9221 6866; www.cathaypacific.com.au.
Emirates: Level 2, 181 St Georges Terrace, tel: 08-9322 6786; www.emirates.com.
Garuda Indonesia: Level 6, Westfarmers House, 40 The Esplanade, tel: 08-9214 5100; www.garuda-indonesia.com.
Malaysia Airlines: 56 William Street, tel: 08-9263 7007; www.malaysia-airlines.com.
Qantas: 55 William Street, tel: 131 313; www.qantas.com.au.
Royal Brunei: 189 St Georges Terrace, tel: 08-9321 8757; www.bruneiair.com.
Singapore Airlines: 178 St Georges Terrace, tel: 08-9265 0500; www.singaporeair.com.au.
Skywest Airlines: Perth Domestic Airport, tel: 08-9478 9999; www.skywest.com.au.
South African Airways: 68 St Georges Terrace, tel: 08-9216 2200; www.saairways.com.au.
Thai Airways: 250 St Georges Terrace, tel: 08-9488 9200; www.thaiairways.com.
Virgin Blue: tel: 136 789; www.virginblue.com.au

FURTHER READING

A Short History of Australia, by Charles Manning Clark. Macmillan A definitive work.
The Fatal Shore, by Robert Hughes, is an epic that follows and records the fate of 160,000 men, women and children transported to Australia.
The People of Perth, by C T Stannage, highlights the characters whose influence did most to develop and shape Perth, from the earliest days to the late 1970s.
Poor Fellow My Country, by Xavier Herbert. A massive novel set in northern Australian Aboriginal community, this masterpiece also traces the steps that produced today's Australia.
The Australian Modern Oxford Dictionary. Oxford University Press.

Left: surf carnival competition at Leighton Beach

The travel guides that replace a tour guide – now better than ever with more listings and a fresh new design

INSIGHT
Pocket Guides

Insight Pocket Guides pioneered a new approach to guidebooks, introducing the concept of the authors as "local hosts" who would provide readers with personal recommendations, just as they would give honest advice to a friend who came to stay. They also included a full-size pull-out map.

Now, to cope with the needs of the 21st century, new editions in this growing series are being given a new look to make them more practical to use, and restaurant and hotel listings have been greatly expanded.

INSIGHT GUIDES

The world's largest collection of visual travel guides

Now in association with

Discovery CHANNEL

credits

ACKNOWLEDGEMENTS

Photography	**Glyn Genin** *with*
Pages 10, 121/B, 13, 14, 15, 16	**Coo-ee Historical Picture Library**
53	**Aquarium of Western Australia** (AQWA)
26T, 28	**Vic Waters**
32T, 39, 40, 51	**Western Australia Tourist Commission**
Title Page	**Glyn Genin**
Front Cover	**Cary Wolinsky/Colourific**
Back Cover	**Glyn Genin**
Cartography	**Berndtson & Berndtson**

INDEX